If You Were
PRESIDENT

★★★★★ *If You Were*
PRESIDENT
Volume I ★★★★★★★★★★★

B. J. MILLER

ISBN: 978-1-4834-0255-0 (e)
ISBN: 978-1-4834-0256-7 (sc)
ISBN: 978-1-4834-0257-4 (hc)

Library of Congress Control Number: 2013912609

Lulu Publishing Services rev. date: 7/23/2013

ENERGY

The biggest waste of energy in the world is the waste of human energy.

Intellect, when combined with a big ego, gets in the way of common sense.

Before you make a decision, weigh both the short-term effects and the long term effects.

B. J. Miller

TABLE OF CONTENTS

INTRODUCTION

On a cold Minnesota winter night I ran out of reading material. A search of my bookshelves produced an old yellowed copy of *Mainspring*, a book with a copyright in 1947. I vaguely remember reading this book when I was just a teenager.

The focus of *Mainspring* was the concept of human energy. The book stated that human energy combined with individual freedom was the key to America's success as a nation. Only in America were people able to own land and other productive assets. In other countries around the world only the rich or the government could own productive assets. If you own something, you have the incentive to improve it and even profit from it.

Our government today has wandered far from the principles of our founding fathers. Lately, I fear that the president and the congress are completely lost. They have forgotten "by the people, for the people, and of the people." The people are the hardworking US citizens that forge our great economy.

The focus of this book will be human energy and how it is applied. Specifically, we need to reduce the size of our federal government because a lot of the human energy applied is actually counterproductive. Please take notes as you read this book, as a Volume II will be written by you and other readers. Send your ideas and comments about what you would do if you were president to the address listed in this book. Do not send e-mails or text messages as the effort required to write and mail your ideas will show you are sincere in your submittals. When your ideas are published in Volume II you will be given full credit in the text published. Propose some legislation or actions that would improve the standard of living of all American citizens.

There are two basic theories in play. Each theory has its proponents that fight to prove that their theory is the correct one. One theory is that resources are limited, and the resources that exist must be redistributed for the benefit of all the people or be saved for future generations. The other theory is that resources are unlimited. There are enough resources for everyone and we will never run out because technology will prevail in providing acceptable substitutes. Therefore, you do not need to redistribute resources from the haves to the have-nots.

I firmly believe that resources are unlimited. I base my opinion on the idea that technology has advanced to the point where man can enjoy unlimited resources if he works hard to develop what the earth provides.

Think about the basic necessities of life today and why they are unlimited. Food and water are really basic, and technology has made the supplies unlimited. It is difficult to transport the basics to where they are needed but it can be done. Nuclear power, the sun, and the wind can provide all the electricity we will ever need. Electricity can replace petroleum in the very near future. So there is no reason to consider oil as a limited resource. We even have the technology to remove the salt from the ocean to provide fresh drinking water for people. The one resource you cannot replace is the human resource, and the energy of millions of people is being wasted today.

This book will show how the government chipped away at our standard of living. For many people the government destroyed their hope of a better life so they just gave up. Many people now believe that no matter how hard you work you just can't get ahead. I hope this book makes you think deeper than you ever have about what the government needs to do to restore hope and faith for a better future. I mean the near future, like next year or the year after. There is hope!

A person need only look at our inner-city areas to see how serious our problems—like widespread unemployment—are becoming. People living in the inner-city neighborhoods don't own anything and can't find meaningful employment and therefore do not have any incentive to improve their lot. They have lost hope and just depend on the government to continue their existence. The middle-class workers now struggle to maintain what little they own. Many of them have given up in the last few years and have lost their homes and all their equity. The remaining middle-class workers cannot support the huge number of people that are no longer working. Human energy should not be wasted like it is, but should be applied to productive activities if our nation is to remain the greatest nation in the world.

If you were president, what would you do? The objective of this book is to stimulate you to think and respond with proposals to set our government on the right track to economic success for millions of struggling citizens. Please help me obtain this objective.

When Volume II is published it will be sent to every senator of every state. The president will definitely get a copy.

YOU HAVE BEEN ELECTED

Wow! Now that you are president, what are you to do? Right away you should be grateful to the electorate and the voters. You are now the leader of all the people, and you need to remember that any legislation you propose should benefit all the people, not just some specific segment of the population. Special interest groups or minorities are not entitled to anything special. If all the people do not benefit from your decisions, then you need to make different decisions.

You will have a couple of months to prepare for your term of office. Establish your principles and morals by writing down what you intend to accomplish for the people. Set some objectives, such as the following:

1. Improve the standard of living for all Americans.
2. Reduce federal spending.
3. Strengthen social security.
4. Revise individual income taxes.
5. Pass a balanced budget.
6. Enhance military capabilities.

7. Improve morality in the United States and among politicians.
8. Ensure citizens can own assets and prosper.
9. Create an environment where government really helps people succeed.
10. Train our workforce for productive activities.
11. Right some past wrongs.
12. Increase federal revenue without increasing taxes.
13. Raise the minimum wage.
14. Calculate inflation properly.
15. Manage the debt and the money supply to increase the value of the dollar.
16. Take care of veterans.
17. Impose a new draft.

The list could be longer, but you only have four to eight years. Now you need to identify and hire the right people to help you accomplish your objectives. Hire people based on their ethics, morals, and accomplishments. Hire only people that are dedicated to the citizens that they are really working for.

So where do you find the right people to hire? Forget about lawyers, professors, and professional politicians. They have already created a big mess. I love this old joke:

Question: What is one lawyer at the bottom of the ocean?
Answer: A good start!

Hire some ordinary people, some businessmen, and some retired military personnel. There are companies like the USAA (United Services Automobile Association) insurance company that have very excellent executives who could do an outstanding job running federal agencies.

If you were president, what would you do? An objective of this book is to stimulate you to think and respond with proposals to set our government on the right track to economic success for millions of struggling citizens. The next president cannot succeed without the help of the Senate and the House of Representatives. God willing, they will all find a way to work together for the common good instead of trying to satisfy their own self-interests.

Write down some objectives that the president and the Congress should achieve.

EXECUTIVE ORDERS

Presidential executive orders should only be used in matters of national defense or other military emergencies. Everything else should go through Congress. As commander in chief, it is definitely appropriate to use executive orders to direct military action, as there is not always time to go through Congress.

Past and current presidents have seemed okay with holding closed-door meetings with staff and congressional leaders in discussing domestic issues. I believe that presidents should spend a lot more time directly addressing the entire House of Representatives and the entire Senate and do so in a public format. That way the citizens can see exactly what everybody is trying to accomplish. The pork riders on bills should be eliminated. Pork usually benefits only a few people to the detriment of everybody else. One agenda at a time, without a bunch of negotiated goodies, should be addressed.

All these presidential orders on domestic issues remind me of a dictatorship or a communistic form of government. Anyone that likes socialism or communism, which at one time were the same thing, is welcome to move to a country that embraces that form of government.

When Nancy Pelosi stated, "We have to pass the (health care) bill so you can find out what's in it", I almost blew a gasket. Nice attitude for a representative. She thinks like a dictator who doesn't care if her own people starve to death. If we allow executive orders on domestic issues, we are promoting a dictatorship.

What do you think?

INCREASE FEDERAL REVENUE

The first thing the politicians think of is how to tax people and businesses. Taxing businesses is also taxing the US citizens, because the companies just increase their prices to the consumers. There are other ways to increase revenues. My outlook is that if the government does increase revenues, it needs to reduce spending and reduce individual taxes at the same time.

According to the History Channel there may be over 147 million troy ounces of gold at Fort Knox. There is also gold stored in New York and in Denver. Our government probably only paid twenty dollars an ounce for most of this gold. It is time to sell some of the gold in 2013, and use the funds to reduce the principal on the national debt. We can't eat gold, or fuel our cars with gold.

Land is a great asset, but if not properly managed, the resources of the land are wasted. The federal government is really good at wasting resources. When storms blow down a hundred thousand acres of mature trees, the government won't let anyone harvest the timber. This happened more than once across Minnesota and other states. There are millions of acres upon which the government will not allow selective harvesting. The fully mature trees just die and rot away. Idle land could just be sold and be put in private hands where the land could become productive. Sell some land and use the money to reduce the national debt.

We should tax all imports from foreign countries and forget about free trade. Why? Because the foreign countries always cheat. They steal our technology and ignore pollution control. They use prison labor, slave labor, and underpaid workers to produce cheaper goods on the sweat of poor souls who are nearly starving. It is really stupid to buy goods from foreign countries when American factories are disappearing. We can make everything we need right here in the good old United States. Foreign countries can build their own internal economies by allowing their own people to increase their standard of living.

Providing military assistance to other countries without some compensation is foolhardy. We protect Saudi Arabia, South Korea, and Kuwait at almost no cost to them. They should pay for everything, as they have the money and the oil to do so. We saved Kuwait but didn't get any discount on oil prices. Iraq and Afghanistan should also pay for some of the help they received. Americans cannot afford to pay for all these countries, as our national debt clearly shows.

If we stop borrowing money, we won't need to pay interest on so much debt. This is the same as increasing revenue, as the funds we have can be applied to a productive activity. The government has the ability to collect money in advance of a project and rathole some of the money before they start a new project or program. However, federal and local governments rarely save up a down payment. You and I are usually required to have a down payment before we buy a car, boat, or house. We need legislation to require the government to set aside funds prior to buying, building, or implementing new programs.

I love the expression, "Drill, baby, drill." Canada drilled its way out of debt, and the United States could do the same. We could wipe out the national debt and increase the standard of living in about five years if we drilled like crazy. Yes, you need to build refineries too! Saving oil for some undefined future period doesn't make sense because technology will negate the need for all that oil in the future. We are alive now and only live for so long. Why should people suffer now? Foreign countries have bled us dry by selling us oil at excessive prices. This is an economic war, and we have not fought back. Drill, baby, drill! Flood the damn market with cheap oil and gas for everyone. A huge amount of revenue would come in so we could improve the lives of all US citizens. In Kuwait people get free training, free college, and free housing. Guess who pays for this!

You can see from the information provided by the Department of the Interior (see appendices) that there are over one billion acres that the US government could sell. If you think the Bureau of Land Management (BLM) properly manages land, you should read the story that follows:

In Nevada I received a permit to hunt mule deer on Mount Grafton. It was a beautiful place considering it was surrounded by desert. Three little springs emerged on the west slope of the mountain. There was watercress in the springs that really enhanced my sandwich. The sagebrush was over knee-high, and grass was everywhere. A cattle ranch nearby had been abandoned. On top of the mountain were pine trees and cedar trees. At forty-five hundred feet, out came two big bucks. I was hiding inside a twelve-foot cedar tree. One shot and the buck dropped dead. The other buck ran away. My son was with me, and we celebrated a successful hunt. In the evening we saw a big herd of about twenty deer running through the sagebrush. A couple years later I was lucky enough to get another permit for Mount Grafton. The BLM had issued grazing permits for the area since I was last there. All the vegetation was gone. Even most of the cedar trees were eaten by sheep and cattle. The three springs were stomped into little mud holes full of cattle dung. There were not any deer anywhere. The sheep and cattle were too numerous and had ruined the entire west side of the mountain. We moved to the next mountain range to the north and found it devoid of vegetation. There were sheepherders and dogs that came from foreign countries to shepherd the big flocks of sheep that ate everything in sight. Again, all the deer were gone. Evidently the BLM does not know that wildlife does not like sheep and wildlife will totally leave the area where sheep are grazing. So much for land stewardship by the BLM! All this land was public land. I'll bet you that all those lamb chops were shipped overseas.

Your thoughts on raising revenue:

REDUCE FEDERAL SPENDING

It could be so easy to reduce spending that Congress and the president should truly be embarrassed. Foreign aid would be number one on my list, because our national debt is too high and our trade balance is terrible. We could easily cut foreign aid by one third. We are giving money to our enemies in many cases.

A couple of federal agencies could disappear and no one would notice their demise. The Department of Education could be eliminated and be replaced by four people at the US Treasury. All that needs to be done is to write fifty-one checks per year. The states and DC can take it from there. I would also eliminate 25 percent of the Department of Commerce. Other agencies could easily be reduced, as many of their employees just shuffle papers between their offices without accomplishing anything. At 50,000 employees the Department of State could be cut by 10,000 employees by closing some consulates around the world. Why keep our people in countries that hate us, and where our people are not safe? If those countries want to contact us they can come over here, use the phone, or use their computers to conduct their business.

Health and Human Services (HHS) had 73,000 employees in 2011 and in 2013 they are expected to have over 76,000 full-time equivalents. Thousands of these people sit in offices in DC. How can those employees help anyone from their office building in Washington? I would cut this agency down to about 50,000 employees. If the agencies work cannot be done with 50,000 people, which is 1000 people per state, then they need to cut a few programs. Some of their programs are mentioned elsewhere in this book. Remember, the states and counties also have people working on these programs.

Housing and Urban Development (HUD) is another big hog. Here is a lot more people just pushing paper and not accomplishing anything physical. How many years does it take to provide public housing? Seems like after all these years we would have a big enough inventory of housing to where we could now cut this program by about 50 percent.

The EPA is out of control. We need all new legislation for this outfit. The EPA should be restricted to the Clean Water Act and that's it. The states can handle everything else. So cut this outfit by 50 percent and get rid of the crazy scientists and mad hatters. Take a look at the EPA budget in the appendices and see how big it has grown. You will be amazed.

The Department of Energy (DOE) also needs a house cleaning. This Department does a great job screwing up the energy industry. I have worked for this agency and I guarantee you that 20 percent of their people just cause extra work for the 80 percent that are actually doing something worth doing. The Peter Principle is really in play in this agency with hundreds of incompetent managers directing people to do paperwork that doesn't need to be done. At one time the DOE was involved with underground nuclear testing. DOE spent hundreds of millions annually on this activity. That activity is gone so why didn't their budget decrease by hundreds of millions?

Another cost-saving measure would be to cut welfare payments. Politically no one wants to touch this issue. The hell with politics. A lot of people are comfortable with living on welfare in their subsidized housing. They should not be comfortable. I believe in helping out but not to the point where people are comfortable and happy with their status quo. We need time and money limits on welfare payments so people know they have to improve their lot by a certain time because the free ride will come to a stop. There is a huge waste of human energy when people are allowed to stay on welfare for twenty years or more. Start now by cutting welfare payments by 1 percent a year for the next five years. A time limit should be imposed, such as: you are only allowed food stamps for thirty-six months out of each five-year period. A record of all welfare benefits for each person should be accumulated and after $200,000 you are off all welfare programs.

Some of the money saved by the cuts mentioned above could be applied to building training centers and paying for training classes for people that don't have employable skills.

Can you think of some big cost savings? You better think hard because all these thousands of government people can't seem to come up with even a small amount of savings. What are your ideas?

THE SERVICE ECONOMY

For many years now the US economy has been evolving to become a service economy instead of a production economy. I can't remember any of the country's financial gurus saying that this would be a bad thing. A service economy is not only bad; it is a horrible thing. Going back in time a little, the United States became very successful because we were production-oriented. We took plentiful natural resources, added human energy, and produced goods and food way beyond our needs. The excess could be sold to other countries and because there was excess, the prices of goods was reasonable for everyone. Everybody's standard of living and quality of life were vastly improved.

Where are the factories and smelters of yesteryear? The factories and productive facilities are now in foreign countries for a variety of reasons. Professors were advising companies to move overseas to increase short-term profits. I attended a master's course at the University of Las Vegas, and the professor just pounded into the students the advantages of moving the production facilities outside the US borders. Finally, I couldn't take it any longer and asked him during class if he had any children and grandchildren.

He answered, "Yes." Then I asked him where his offspring were going to find a job. He didn't have an answer. If you build a Buick in Mexico the low-income Mexican workers cannot afford to buy the Buicks they are making. If the professors' offspring do not have jobs they can't buy a Buick either. There are long-term problems when you go for short-term profits. You need to pay wages commensurate with the work being done and with the cost of the items the workers are producing. If your employees cannot afford the things they are making then your product is just not going to sell and eventually you will go out of business. I received a B for this marketing class instead of an A because I continued to argue with him for the rest of the semester. He didn't like my arguments because he couldn't justify what he was teaching. What other bad information are our kids learning?

Solution: We need to return to being a nation that applies resources to produce goods and equipment. If government regulations are in the way, we need to eliminate them. If foreign countries are dumping goods on us at lower costs we need to tax their imports to level the playing field. We don't need finished goods from China and Japan as we can produce everything we need right here in the US. Do you remember when the Japanese dumped steel and ruined our steel industry? By the way, how green is it to ship our iron ore across the ocean and have the foreign steel and iron shipped back here? Imagine all the fuel wasted by those ships.

Your ideas and notes:

STIMULUS SPENDING

Stimulus spending is okay if the money is spent wisely. Hoover Dam is a good example of wise stimulus spending. President Obama really missed an opportunity during the last four years. He had a ton of stimulus money but he scattered the money all over the place and didn't create any lasting legacy. He missed out on a claim to fame. That money could have been applied to a huge national project to benefit all citizens far into the future. Obama could have built a national college and training center. He could have built a few refineries. He could have built an aqueduct to bring water to the Southwest. Instead, he put his name on Solyrindra and other failed projects. The only benefit of the Obama stimulus that I am aware of is some roads that were repaired. I am aware of the roads because they put huge signs up touting the stimulus.

Some other things the stimulus could have financed would be steel mills and brick factories. High speed trains to carry people and cargo could have been built. How much fuel would be saved if you moved more people and goods by train instead of by plane or semi-truck?

Steel and iron built the industrial America that was so successful in the past. The Japanese flooded the market with cheap steel and drove some of our steel mills out of business. Now, the EPA would probably not allow the construction of a steel mill unless they spent $200 million on smoke reduction. Steel and iron are critical to national defense. You could even say steel is green because you can make 2x4s of steel and buildings of steel, and reduce the number of trees you cut down. Remember, the three little pigs built houses and the big bad wolf blew two of the houses down. Well, here we are today building houses of wood and vinyl and the big bad wolf is at the door. More steel and more bricks means cheaper steel and bricks and better-built homes. It also creates more skilled jobs that pay well.

Another good use of stimulus money would be to build about ten new nuclear power plants. The Al Gores of the world have everybody worried about nuclear waste and claim that there isn't any place to put it. They are wrong. I worked for the Department of Energy in Nevada and I can attest to the ease of disposing of nuclear waste. At the Nevada Test Site (NTS) they drilled holes as large as six feet in diameter right through solid rock. The holes were over a thousand feet deep, and nuclear device tests were exploded in those holes after the holes were plugged with magnetite and cement. Today there is still hot nuclear waste down there, and it does not migrate very far. The waste that is down there is 1000 times worse than waste from expended fuel rods. There are some holes out there that were never used, and more holes could be drilled. Waste from nuclear plants could be containerized and be put in the holes. The holes could then be plugged and capped. All we need is a president with the guts to transport the waste to Nevada. Remember, the current waste is stored in pools of water right next to all the major rivers like the Mississippi. Major rivers usually sit on earthquake faults, and a lot of big cities get their drinking water out of those rivers.

In 1933 Robert W. Johnson of Johnson & Johnson wrote a letter to President Roosevelt at a time when 10 million people were out of work. The letter set forth some important economic principles:

1. "We will have to live within our means, and this is also the case with all levels of government. America has spent more than its income until we have reached a point where our public and private credit has collapsed. All budgets should be balanced, in fact."
2. "International debts should be reduced."
3. "Wages should be increased and hours should be decreased."
4. "A government can make its citizens poor but no government to date has been able to make its citizens rich. Taking from those who have and distributing to those who have not is the expediency of economic suicide. It is obviously unfair to tax the few for the benefit of the many. Inheritance tax should be minimized or eliminated. There is no greater incentive in life than working for the benefit of one's children."

Mr. Johnson realized that high unemployment was a waste of human energy. Welfare recipients are really a huge waste of human energy. People need to be trained for the jobs that are available. We need limits on welfare and unemployment to get people back to work. Extending benefits is not the way to go. The way to go is to make people go to training and then go to work.

For a couple of years the federal government didn't even have a budget. Shame on the senate of this country. In 1935 Mr. Johnson wrote another letter to Congress stating: "We shall have no rest, peace, prosperity or happiness in this country until man and women are back on jobs again. Until the problem is solved we will only see a continuation of the tragic disorder, waste and human misery of the past five years. I just hope we don't have another five years of high unemployment or there will be tragic disorder in the United States."

If you were to stimulate the economy with $700 billion, what would you spend the money on?

Please suggest some solutions to the unemployment problem:

USURY

Good old boy President Carter did away with the federal usury law. This was a good law that protected US citizens. Sometime after the law was repealed, the interest rates on mortgages went as high as 16 percent. Ordinary folks lost a lot of money because this law was eliminated.

In Minnesota and other states, there are usury laws, but they are too much in favor of the lenders. Poor people getting small, unsecured loans pay as much as 32 percent interest plus an application fee. Some of the loans are for emergency medical services. Isn't it funny that the people that can least afford it must pay higher rates than other people? Today, with interest rates at an all time low, some credit cards charge 21 percent interest. This is robbery as those companies can borrow from the federal government at about a 2 percent rate.

If you were president would you protect people by passing a new usury law? And what percent would be fair? Seems like even Jesus didn't like money-lenders. Maybe the government should cap the rates at 11 percent above the treasury rates. Mortgage rates should be capped at a maximum of 9 percent.

About 1983 I assumed a conventional mortgage in Minnesota at 8 percent. I lived there two years and paid my mortgage on time every month. In Minnesota it was legal to assume a conventional loan. The federal government, for some unknown reason, had a law that forbade the assumption of a conventional loan. The banks in Minnesota went to court because interest rates had risen to 15 or 16 percent and the banks didn't want people to be able to sell their homes at 8 percent with a conventional assumption. The banks were greedy. The court ruled in favor of the banks and did not grandfather anyone that had already assumed a loan. The bank called me and said I had to refinance at over 15 percent. I refused to pay 15 percent on a mortgage I now had at 8 percent. I was required to deed the house over to the bank and lost all my equity in my home, and my family had to move out of the house. The only reason the conventional loans are not assumable is to protect the banks and allow greedy banks to make more money. The house I lost sat empty for over a year, so the bank lost money and I lost money. Because the bank was greedy, we both lost money.

Here we are today and people are being foreclosed on again and have lost all the equity in their homes. The government protected the banks again, at the expense of the homeowners. If the government had let the homeowners refinance at today's low rates, a lot of the people could have kept their homes. Instead, the government bails out AIG, Fannie Mae and Ginne Mae. The citizens lose twice. People lost their equity and the taxpayers bailed out the government, the banks, the insurance companies, and mortgage companies. This was probably the biggest theft of people's money in history.

Your comments and ideas:

MONEY SUPPLY

Other nations have always coveted US dollars because our currency and our government were more stable than theirs. The more money you print, the less the value of that money. Our currency is not backed by gold any more. It is just crazy to print more money just so you can spend more, and really crazy to print money when you have a big national debt. On top of this we are printing money to give away to other countries. Even a raving lunatic would not devalue the currency to give money away. We definitely need a congressional limit on the expansion of the money supply. How fast can you spend a $100 bill today? One hundred bucks bought a lot of food about twenty years ago. Today $450 buys a lot of food.

Fifty years ago I bought gas for twenty-five cents a gallon and got a free water glass. Yesterday I paid $3.74 a gallon for gas. In one lifetime gas costs fifteen times what it used to cost. Some of this increase is due to printing money without a comparable increase in the gross national product.

Eventually, if you keep printing too much money, the other countries in the world won't want our dollars anymore. They will dump our money for some other currency or they will trade it for gold or silver. If this happens our economy will crash.

The money supply needs to be based on the gross national product or some other economic indicator of a strong economy. If we don't limit the money supply we will need a wheelbarrow full of money to buy bread, like it was in Germany at one time.

One reason our currency is retaining value today is that other countries are printing more money than they should. The other reason is that we have a stable government with a strong military.

What are your thoughts on this subject?

LEGISLATION

It is time for new rules on legislation. Any legislation over five pages in length should be rejected or tabled indefinitely. A good rule would be: In order to pass five pages of new legislation you must get rid of twenty-five pages of old legislation. You need to know that for every page of legislation some agency will write a hundred pages of rules and regulations and interpretations. Our constitution is only about sixteen pages long. The Declaration of Independence is only about three pages long. Obamacare is thousands of pages.

I have spent hundreds of hours reading federal regulations, because at the time I was being paid to audit federal programs. I nearly went out of my mind. As you read the regulations you are continually referred to other sections and other regulations until, after many hours, you get lucky and find the answer you were looking for. I realize that government lawyers need some work to do. But instead of focusing on how long and complicated the lawyers can make something, let's teach them to eliminate regulations and simplify the ones that are really necessary. Some millions of hours of human energy could be better spent on more productive activities.

Trust me: There are too many federal rules and regulations. You will not find any common-sense guidelines in all those writings. Go to the library and read some of the federal agency regulations in the CFR (codified federal regulations). You will be amazed at the complexity.

Over the years various politicians have passed special legislation for new programs that only benefit special interest groups. The programs do not provide benefits to all citizens. They did this just to get votes. Today we are supporting hundreds of these programs with our tax dollars. Many of the programs, according to the GAO, are duplicating the effort of other programs. We just cannot afford to finance all these programs. Legislation needs to be repealed.

Your Comments:

THE NEW DRAFT

Don't be scared by the word "draft." The new draft would not include sending your child into combat. The new draft would be for both young men and young women who were not enrolled in school after high school. It doesn't hurt anyone to serve his or her country for two years. A sense of pride in yourself, pride in your country, and a sense of accomplishment can be achieved.

The new draft would allow draftees to choose between job corps, military service or a federal apprenticeship with a federal agency. All assignments would include training programs for the first six months. The young people could learn skills that they might otherwise never experience. A lot of public works projects could be completed utilizing the energy of the draftees. Cities could be cleaned up and parks could be improved.

A lot of young people are sort of lost after high school and they really don't know what to do with themselves. Many high school graduates are not even fully mature yet. Normally the only jobs available for these youngsters are low paying part-time jobs. After all, you don't really even have a résumé upon graduating from high school. A two-year delay for most young people would give them time to develop job skills.

The military option could include two options:

1. combat-related, and
2. non-combat positions.

The military needs a lot of support people behind the lines of combat. Many young people could learn a lot working on US military bases by helping the military personnel with their duties.

Social services could definitely use a lot of young talent to clean up inner-city neighborhoods and help out elderly people. Some of the young people could be trained to provide security services for public housing projects and parks.

Would you like a draft that trained your kids and gave them skills?

Comments:

INFLATION FORMULA

Everybody knows the government calculates inflation percentages based on an improper formula. Yet no one takes action to correct this inequity. Inflation is different for the middle class than it is for rich people or poor people. If groceries and gas prices increase, the rich could care less. More than likely the rich will get bigger dividends on their stock holdings to offset most price increases. The poor get food stamps and subsidized rent, so they really don't care about the inflation rate either. Inflation should be calculated based on the middle-class range of income. The rate should include increases in all costs.

Energy price increases and food price increases are not even considered in the government's formula, but these items are now major budget line items for the middle class. Twenty years ago I didn't even budget for food and gas because they were both relatively inexpensive compared to my income. Today, both these items are budgeted for.

People on social security really get clobbered over the years when inflation is understated by the government. The increases in payments do not keep up with increases in living costs. The disparity is compounded as years go by. I estimate that in the last three years people on social security have lost about 6 percent of their spending power. That chicken that provided two meals has to provide three meals now. I get tired of chicken soup after awhile.

If inflation continues to be understated for another five years I guarantee you will not live comfortably on your social security. If the government thinks they save money by understating inflation, they are wrong. More people will just go down and apply for food stamps, so the government won't save a dime.

President Obama's 2014 budget proposes to further reduce the inflation factor in order to reduce increases in social security payments. This reduction will end up applying to the raises that nearly everyone will expect in the future. Changing the formula again will hurt everybody. This is exactly opposite of what should happen. Change the formula to reflect actual inflation related to the middle-class salary range. We need to take actions that increase the standard of living instead of decreasing the standard of living. Social security recipients are always characterized as being on a fixed income. They are not on a fixed income. Social security retirees are on a declining income because the inflation rate is always understated. They cannot afford further reductions in their spending power.

Would you propose changing the inflation formula?

IMPROVE THE STANDARD OF LIVING

There is only one way to improve the standard of living. You must create good-paying jobs that produce goods for consumption. The federal government has to promote the creation of jobs by facilitating the proper environment. Less regulation and tax incentives definitely improve the environment. A big factor is foreign trade. We need to restrict the amount of goods that come here from other countries. Anything they can make overseas we can make here in the United States. We have both human resources and natural resources that are currently underutilized. It is okay to import raw materials but not finished goods.

People want to label certain policies with names like protectionism. Protectionism is not a bad word or a bad policy. What is wrong with protectionism if you and your family members have good paying jobs because of it? There isn't a lot of time left. The last five years have been wasted and it takes time to build factories and train people. Providing training to Americans should be a big priority. Training for productive jobs could greatly reduce the welfare rolls. Wouldn't it be cheaper to train somebody for a year than pay them welfare for ten years? People need to work to feel good about themselves. Right now there is a shortage of welders and truck drivers in this country. I'm sorry if you don't like that kind of work but many of us have had jobs we didn't like. We did the jobs anyway to support ourselves and our families.

The government needs to give up some of the land they are holding. Land is needed for the expansion of the economy. Some of the land could be farmed, some contains timber to be harvested, some is suitable for drilling for oil and gas and on some land we could build refineries or power plants. Sell some land and the development will create thousands of jobs.

Welfare payments and extended unemployment do not increase the standard of living for anyone. Human energy is wasted and once it is wasted you cannot get it back. The longer people stay on these programs the less likely they are to ever go back to work. In order to get these benefits you should be required to take vocational training. A national vocational training center could be built in Omaha in the middle of the country. If you gear the training to jobs that are available, the students could go to work in a short time.

What would you do to increase the standard of living? Don't let SOL stand for shit-out-of-luck.

CHARITY VERSUS WELFARE

Charity, of course, is a good thing, but there needs to be a limit to it. It makes us feel good when we personally donate directly to a charitable cause. When the federal government gives away my tax dollars as welfare I don't feel so good about it. Why does the federal government get to decide where my money for charity goes? I read the Constitution and I didn't see where the federal government gets its authority for giving away money. I hate it when tax dollars are given to foreign countries because, simply, you cannot buy friends. History has shown that foreign countries often become our enemies and despise us for giving them money and weapons.

The American College Dictionary gives us some good definitions. A welfare state is one in which the welfare of the people in such matters as social security, health and education, housing, and working conditions is the responsibility of the government. Do we want to be known as a welfare state? I argue with our social security being called welfare because workers and businesses pay into the fund. The survivor portion of social security is welfare. Charity is defined as the private or public relief of unfortunate or needy persons: a benevolent feeling towards those in need. I would rather our nation be known as a charitable one instead of known as a welfare state.

I have an unusual solution for this situation. On our tax forms there should be a line where we could designate that 10 percent of the taxes we pay be donated to a specific charity or country of our personal choice. You could even designate food stamps or public housing or cancer research or whatever organization you wished. The choice would then be ours. Again, where is the authority for the federal government to give away our hard-earned money?

What do you think?

THE REPUBLIC

Everybody thinks of the United States as being a democracy. A democracy is government by the people. Supreme power rests with the people. A democracy is social equality for all the people. A democracy is not financial equality. This country is also a republic.

A republic is a state in which the supreme power rests in the body of citizens entitled to vote.

A patriot is a person who loves his country. A patriot defends his country. One way to defend our country is to educate people about the founding principles. We cannot stand idly by while socialism sneakily invades our founding principles to promote communism. Socialism is a system that advocates the vesting of the ownership and control of the means of production, capital, and land in the community as a whole. In other words, the government owns and controls everything. In America we believe in private ownership and control. Under Communism all economic activity is conducted by a totalitarian state dominated by a single political party.

How close are we getting to being communists? Just look at the amount of economic activity that is controlled by the federal government today. Over $16 trillion in debt and the printing presses are running out more dollars. On TV they say that the debt is over $50,000 for every man, woman and child in the US. The debt is going higher each day. God help us! In God we trust!

US CONSTITUTION
(GROSSLY ABBREVIATED)

Article 1

Section 7   All bills for raising revenue shall originate in the House of Representatives.

Section 8   Congress shall have power to lay and collect taxes, duties, imposts and excises, to pay the debts and provide for the common defense and general welfare of the United States. The power to borrow money and regulate commerce with foreign nations and among the several states and with the Indian tribes. The power to coin money, regulate the value thereof and fix the standard of weights and measures. To establish post offices. To declare war. To raise and support an army and navy. To make all laws which shall be necessary for carrying into execution all powers vested by this constitution.

Section 9   No bill of attainder or ex post facto law shall be passed. No money shall be drawn from the treasury but in consequence of appropriations made by law.

Article 2

Section 2   The President shall be commander-in-chief. He shall have power to grant reprieves and pardons. He shall from time to time give to the congress information of the state of the union. The president and vice-president and all civil officers shall be removed from office for, and conviction of, treason, bribery, or other high crimes and misdemeanors.

Article 3

Section 1   The judicial power shall be vested in one supreme court and in such inferior courts as the congress may ordain and establish.

Article 4

Section 2   The citizens of each state shall be entitled to all privileges and immunities of citizens in the several states.

Amendment 1 Freedom of speech and religion. The right of the people to peaceably assemble and to petition the government for a redress of grievances.

Amendment 2 The right of the people to keep and bear arms shall not be infringed.

Amendment 4 The right of the people to be secure in their persons, houses, papers and effects, against unreasonable searches and seizures.

Amendment 9 The enumeration in the Constitution, or certain rights, shall not be construed to deny or disparage others retained by the people.

Amendment 10 The powers not delegated to the United States are reserved to the States or to the people.

This grossly abbreviated Constitution is just for the purpose of reference for the reading of this book.

VOLUME II
IF YOU WERE PRESIDENT

Volume II will be written by all the readers of Volume I that submit their personal ideas and thoughts of what they would do if they were president. Volume II will be subtitled "The People Speak Out."

Please send your input to the address below and indicate whether you want your name and city listed in Volume II. I think people deserve credit for their input; however, if you wish to remain anonymous, indicate that on your submission. Criticisms are okay if they are positive in nature.

Please send all comments and ideas by November 30th, 2014.

B.J. Miller
P.O. Box 394
Milaca, MN 56353

Thank you for your interest in Volume I and for your input to Volume II.

THE ELECTION PROCESS

The Constitution states: "Each state shall appoint, in such manner as the legislature thereof may direct, a Number of Electors." These electors vote and the person having the greatest number of votes shall be the president. This part of our constitution needs to be changed. The popular vote should determine who becomes president.

If we went by the popular vote we could have major changes in the political parties. Why should a few people determine the Presidency? When there are only two viable candidates we sometimes have to vote for the lesser of two evils. We shouldn't have to vote for the one we believe will do the least harm. Why not have six candidates each four years?

Along with having six candidates, you need to put a limit on how much each of them can spend running for president. Currently, the candidates spend too much money. In the past there was a big deal about campaign reform and since then things have only gotten worse. If there were money limits then more people could afford to run for office and maybe even some sound-minded middle-class citizens could throw their hat in the ring.

All those TV ads don't sway my vote at all. Most ads are negative, which doesn't seem very dignified in relation to the presidency. A little more civility seems to be in order. When they run ads that provide false information they should suffer a financial penalty and be required to run a correction. If they lie about another candidate they should be fined part of the campaign funding. Then, maybe they would be more careful about their facts.

The new controversy is whether you need to provide proof of citizenship to vote. Why not? This is just silly. We need more honesty in our voting and identification will help.

I want my vote to count for something. I want to make a difference. How about you?

Governor Romney and his advisors really blew it when they campaigned. A president is the president of all fifty states. The campaign focused on swing states. I would have focused on all fifty states. California is a good example because they just assumed it would go democratic. So what? You don't give up based on statistics or past history. You try to get all the states no matter what. Governor Romney, a Mormon, should have known better. The Mormons have missions in countries that will never be Christian or Mormon countries, but they go there to try and convert as many people as they can. The Republican Party needs to develop the mission concept. The Democrats are smarter when it comes to campaigning. The Democrats begin years ahead of time to convince—brainwash —children and everybody else that their platform is the only way to go. The Democrats campaign relentlessly all year long, every year. Their mission work never stops and doesn't exclude any state that was historically Republican. Wake up Republicans!

INDIVIDUAL INCOME TAXES

It seems really strange that the people that receive the most benefits from the federal government are the people that don't pay any federal income tax or pay just a tiny amount. Maybe it is time for a flat tax on everyone. Middle-class families with a family income of $50,000 to $100,000 are being pounded to death by state and federal taxes and fees of all kinds. The term *middle class* should probably be replaced with the term *working slaves*.

I'm not sure the founding fathers intended for there to be a federal individual income tax when they wrote the constitution. Before 1909 they didn't have a federal income tax on individuals. If we must have such a tax, let's make it fair and minimize it. Just charge everybody 6 percent of their paycheck and have the employer send the money directly to the Treasury each month. You wouldn't even need to file a return anymore. I realize that this would kill an entire paperwork industry but that industry is totally non-productive anyway so we are better off without it. Save a tree or two. It shouldn't matter if you earn $400 per month or $5,000 per month, as everyone will pay 6 percent of their gross earnings.

All the current reporting and related paperwork will be eliminated and the human energy can be applied to some other more productive activity. On the next page is a sample of a flat tax return.

A lot of congressmen are in favor of a flat tax and so are a lot of citizens, but no one seems to be able to get things changed. Where is the leadership on this issue?

Your ideas:

EXAMPLE OF A FLAT TAX RETURN

2015 US Individual Income Tax Return
Name:
SSN:
Address:

Source of Income	Dollar Amounts Rounded	Rate	Tax
Wages/Salaries	30000	6%	1800
Tips	500	4%	20
Retirement Income			
Private or Government Pensions	10000	5%	500
Social Security	6000	2%	120
IRA and 401K Distributions	8000	5%	400
Interest and Dividends	300	6%	18
Capital Gains	1000	10%	100
Other Income (specify source)	0	6%	0
Total Income and Total Tax	55800		2958

This is what a tax return should look like. I realize some people will lose their paper-pushing jobs and some lawyers will really be miffed. Why waste all that human energy on complex rules and regulations and confusing instructions? You wouldn't need a tax expert anymore and the IRS could reduce the number of employees. This return would remove a lot of stress from people and save time.

Most states have individual income taxes. The state tax might be $2580 so this person would pay a total of $5538 or 10 percent of their gross income. Then we add $2760 for social security and Medicare and another $490 for state sales tax, bringing it to $8788 or 15.75 percent of gross income that is not available to spend supporting a family. There are other taxes and fees in addition to the above.

Under the system in effect today, this family would pay about $6000 in federal income tax instead of $2958 in the above flat tax example.

VIETNAM VETERANS

I have read at least twenty-five books written about the Vietnam War and none of them mentioned Military Payment Certificates (MPCs). Somebody—an idiot—in our government decided that our presence in Vietnam resulted in a lot of inflation, because the piastre (Vietnamese currency) kept going down in value. The politicians directed the military to do something unthinkable. If you were in the military you had to change your American greenbacks for MPCs or face a court martial. You could spend MPCs or piastres but not American money. For $1 you could get 115 MPCs valued at 115 piasters. The rub was that $1 in the money market would get you about 330 piastres. This was done to stabilize the piastre. The problem was it was done by screwing American soldiers out of half of their buying power. How immoral is it to cheat the fighting soldiers out of half of their money? Remember, a lot of the soldiers had been drafted and their pay was very small. This system did not apply to any civilians or contractor employees, so they could change money on the black market and basically save their entire paycheck. A lot of civilians became rich changing American money into piastres and then changing the money back again.

After WWII combat soldiers received a bonus from the federal government. After the Vietnam War the veterans did not get a federal bonus and a lot of men were kicked out of the military as part of a reduction in force (RIF). Well-trained and experienced soldiers were sent home when many of them wanted to stay in the military. Some states were nice enough to give their homeboys a small bonus after the war but in most cases it was only $300 to $500 depending on which state you were from. Remember, the pay for a private in 1969 was about $200 a month. A civilian could earn over $800 per month in 1969.

So, how do you right this wrong? It is almost impossible to calculate the financial impact of the immoral policies because each man was affected to a different degree. The psychological impact of the treatment of Vietnam veterans cannot be quantified. We were all called baby-killers when we got home. Imagine fighting for your country and having six years of service and then being told to go home in two weeks. Your idea may have been to serve twenty years or more and retire with a pension. You may have been very patriotic. Now, you have been crushed. Some soldiers sucked it up and went to school on the GI Bill and others went to live under a bridge in Las Vegas and just went nuts.

Solution: The government owes every Vietnam veteran an apology and a big fat check to them or their survivors.

What do you think?

THE PETER PRINCIPLE PLUS

The federal government has revised the Peter Principle but not in a good way. You remember the theory that in government and in business people are promoted to the level where they are incompetent? There is a new game in town called mentoring.

The new system works very well for the totally incompetent and lazy federal employees. First, you get a job anywhere in the federal government whether or not you are really qualified to do the work. Now, you are totally lost and can't do the job you were assigned. So, you go to the highest manager or supervisor you can get access to and ask them to be your mentor. A little brown-nosing and ego-building will get you a yes. Now, this manager's success depends on your success, so that mentor will ensure that you succeed. When you get an assignment you run to your mentor for advice and the mentor will direct you to someone that knows what to do. Always name-drop who your mentor is. Compliment your mentor profusely and go to the expert that in most instances will do most of the work for you. You put your name and your mentor's name on the product and forget about the expert that really did the work.

Now it is time for your first promotion. Your mentor will gladly support your promotion to make both of you look good. You are still incompetent but at a higher level in the organization. This process can be repeated many times until you have been promoted to a level higher than that of the people that actually did the work. This method even has built-in insurance. If anything goes terribly wrong you can blame the people that did the work. Because you have been successful at scamming the system, your ego has ballooned to where you can now be a mentor. If a major screwup occurs you are safe because your managers and your mentors have promoted you and have sung your praises for years. Your managers will cover your butt to save their own.

Another aspect of this strategy is to be appointed to a team project. A problem arises so a team is assigned to derive a solution. Get yourself assigned to a good team with an excellent team leader. Do very little work for the team, as you are incompetent anyway. When the team is a success you get the same credit as the team members that actually solved the problem. You score points without shooting a basket.

The end product of the mentoring program is a lot of incompetent people making a lot of money for doing nothing. Now you know how to have a successful government career.

Solution: Go back to the old method of hiring the most qualified people and promoting people based on their individual accomplishments. It will be very difficult to change the current environment because there are so many of these incompetent people on the federal payroll today.

Your ideas and comments:

THE 2010 CENSUS

The purpose of the census is to count the people to determine voting districts. Somewhere along the line this purpose has been distorted to include gathering information about alleged minorities and household income and even what sex people are.

I worked for the 2010 Census. What a joke this job was. I went to two weeks of training and then worked two weeks part-time. After two weeks we were told that phase one was finished. They had given us GPS (global positioning) locators, made in a foreign country, and we had to establish a map point for all residences. The GPS only worked sporadically. We knocked on doors and gathered information on an eight-page questionnaire.

A month later I was hired a second time to validate data previously recorded. The data was already about 95 percent accurate. I trained for this position for about a week. I only worked one week part-time and was told we were done. In Minnesota they had hired way too many people and there wasn't that much work to be done. All this activity was very inefficient because we spent more time in training than we did working.

The second phase was ridiculous. If a woman answered the door I was supposed to ask her what sex she was. If the woman said she had a son living there I was supposed to ask what sex her son was. Of course I did not follow my instruction: I just assumed the lady's sex was female. How foolish of me! I kept validating data already collected by someone else and rarely found any mistakes.

A lady came to my home in the country to do census work. Mind you, I had mailed in the forms on time. I live a long ways from town. A few weeks later another woman drove up to ask the same census questions. Thank goodness they didn't ask what sex I was. I told both these ladies I had mailed in my forms and I didn't wish to answer any questions. I wonder if this fiasco occurred in other parts of the country.

Do you have any stories about the 2010 Census? I'll bet you they spent twice what they needed to in order to count people. The government doesn't need all the information they collect. Some of the questions are really an invasion of privacy. Also, why did they need a GPS point for all the private residences? With a little planning the next census could be conducted at half the cost of the 2010 census.

Do you think the government has a right to collect all that information?

THE MINIMUM WAGE

The current minimum wage is a bad joke. A person or family can live better on welfare than they can working for the minimum wage. Why? Because it costs money to go to work and you only bring home about 85 percent of your pay at minimum wage rates.

The way the government calculates inflation is part of the problem. The government always understates the rate of inflation. Reality is distorted by the formula used. The distortion is compounded as years go by. The minimum wage should be about $12.75 per hour for 2013.

An acquaintance works for the Minnesota unemployment agency. He tells me that families make the equivalent of $50,000 per year on assistance plus unemployment.

The *Minneapolis StarTribune* had a good article this year about the minimum wage. In the article the authors, Aaron Sojourrner and Michael Reich, stated that the minimum wage should be $9.80 to $10.55 per hour in Minnesota. They also wrote that in states where the minimum wage has been increased, there was not any loss of jobs. When the wage was increased the businesses stayed in those states and there was not any loss of employment. Match this article with what many of the politicians say about raising the minimum wage. There is a big disconnect. Raising the wage seldom results in price increases because the market and competition determine prices in the United States.

Would the politicians work for $7.50 an hour? Solution: Change the way inflation is calculated and increase the minimum wage to reflect the real cost of living. I maintain that $7.50 an hour is the same as slavery.

The minimum wage should also be indexed to the cost of living in each state. In California or New York City the minimum wage should probably be about $15 an hour. People working for the government are earning $20 to $50 an hour but those same people are telling the rest of the citizens that $8 an hour is okay.

Your ideas and notes: What should be the minimum wage per hour?

MILITARY VETERANS' PENSIONS

The military retirement system needs to be revised. People can serve for five years to fifteen years and through no fault of their own, not earn any retirement benefits for their service to their country.

I had six years of active duty and, when nearing retirement age later in life, I had to pay the government $5,000 so my military service would count towards my social security. After six or seven years of active duty a veteran should be vested in at least a small military pension to be paid to them at age fifty-five. Currently you can get caught up in a reduction in force (RIF) and all the years you spent in the military won't count for any retirement benefits. You can also be discharged just because you didn't attain a higher rank within a specified period. The rub is that you can be a perfect soldier, be patriotic and desire to serve for twenty-five years but be discharged before you qualify for military retirement benefits. This can happen even if all your appraisals were excellent. A veteran of foreign wars should not be treated this way.

Officers are especially vulnerable. If you don't make Major or Lieutenant Colonel within the timeframe specified by the military you can be discharged against your will. This is called *being passed over*. Graduates of the military academies seldom get passed over so they use up all the available higher ranks. As a captain, you can do an excellent job as a commander and still be discharged.

If nothing else, the military should contribute to social security for your years of service. You shouldn't need to pay into social security out of your own pocket.

What do you think?

WAR

The politicians didn't learn anything from the Vietnam conflict. Iraq and Afghanistan are proof again of how foolish it is for us to fight other people's wars for them. Iraq is already going backwards. If these countries don't have the will to fight their own battles then why should good Americans die for people that are not even our friends? The people over there do not share our values and they do not appreciate our sacrifices.

The young handsome son of a preacher slipped off the top of a Huey helicopter and fell flat on his back. I thought for sure he would be severely injured. He jumped up and said "I'm okay." This young man was one of the nicest and smartest men in my detachment. A few days later during a mortar attack he tried to save a friend of his, and he was hit and killed by a mortar round. At the time I wondered why the best of the best have to die. This kid could have done great things in the future. War really sucks!

Before my young mechanic died we were bombarded by mortars and rockets day and night for thirty days. Dau Tieng was a real hot area for a while. Sometimes the artillery unit next to us didn't fire back at the enemy. I went to see the battery commander to ask why he didn't return fire. The artillery commander stated he wasn't authorized to fire into the rubber plantation trees because then we had to pay reparations for killing trees. I became very angry at that explanation. I took a Huey on a test flight and flew over the rubber plantation. Under the trees were shallow depressions where the enemy could lie and fire at us. I had the door gunners shoot up the place and shoot up the field next to the trees. We were able to chase the enemy out of the area and we captured a mortar. At least we had a few days without enemy fire. Great policy: save a tree but kill a soldier.

I got up early as usual one morning and proceeded to the maintenance area when suddenly I heard a freight train coming through the air. I was halfway to the earth when the air filled with wood scraps and debris. The loud explosion noise followed. An enormous rocket we called an ashcan had a direct hit on a latrine behind the maintenance tent. A soldier inside the latrine was blown to pieces. My sergeant was wounded and was screaming so I went to his aid. He was worried about his manhood being gone and was going into shock. I stripped off his uniform and told him his man parts were okay. He relaxed and didn't go fully into shock. He did have tiny holes in his legs and back where shrapnel had penetrated his body. It was only a couple of minutes when the medics arrived and he was taken to safety. He survived. Again, one of the nicest guys was wounded.

I cannot stress enough how serious it is to put young Americans in harm's way. Politicians are just clueless about wars. You can't draw lines on a map and restrict combat operations to only certain areas. When you are attacked you need the flexibility to pursue the enemy wherever he goes and eliminate that enemy as quickly as possible. There isn't always time to ask permission or coordinate with a foreign government. You also need to employ the right weapons right away. In Vietnam they were always establishing no-fire zones and no-fly zones. You just cannot win a war that way, and your own casualties are much higher that way. Personally, I would have bombed North Vietnam into oblivion and then sent troops north of the DMZ to wipe out their army and their will to fight.

Today, we have over 28,000 military personnel in South Korea. For crying out loud, we have been there since the 1940s. Can't the South Koreans train another 20,000 Koreans so we can bring our people home? We could leave some equipment there and fly men over there later if they are ever needed. It would be better if the South Koreans just did their own thing. We had some South Korean soldiers in Vietnam. They were really tough customers. The North Vietnamese were afraid of the Koreans and would always run away from them because they were so brutal in combat.

One of our warrant officer pilots received a message from home that his pregnant wife had a vision he would be killed in Vietnam. She was having a nervous breakdown, which was really bad for the unborn baby. He was allowed to go home on leave to visit his wife. His wife was satisfied with seeing him one more time and he got to watch his child be born. A few days later he was sent back to Dau Tieng. About a week later his chopper was shot down and he made the mistake of surrendering to the Viet Cong. One of the door gunners escaped through the jungle to a small American firebase. The door gunner was just nineteen years old but smart enough to shed his boots and go barefoot so he wouldn't be tracked down. The gunner came to see me. He was all scratched up from the jungle vegetation. I told him he was eligible to go back home but he wanted to stay and help search for the rest of the crew.

We searched for days but didn't find the warrant officer or the crew. A local Vietnamese guy that worked for the CIA said the crew was captured and he would try to buy our people back from the Viet Cong. Everybody chipped in some money, and we sent the guy out to try and get our men back. The Vietnamese came back a week later and told us what happened. The Viet Cong had taken our people to a village where they were mistreated and then killed in front of the villagers. The enemy did this just for propaganda reasons. Did you ever notice that all the POWs that came home were mostly officers that were from camps in North Vietnam? They were mostly pilots that were captured in North Vietnam. All the enlisted men the enemy captured in South Vietnam were just murdered. The enemy claimed they had no knowledge of the Geneva Convention. The enemy also claimed it was too difficult to take prisoners north through the jungle to an interment camp. All their excuses don't sway my opinion. It is murder and a war crime to kill captured prisoners. When

Americans captured enemy soldiers we locked them up in re-education camps where they were treated very well. The South Vietnamese sometimes tortured prisoners, but Americans, to my knowledge, did not mistreat anybody.

Almost every night we had to work late to repair the helicopters for the next day's missions. For every hour you fly a chopper you need to do nine hours of maintenance. One night the sergeant brought in a young mechanic that refused to go out in the pitch-black night to repair a rotor system. The sergeant wanted me to court martial the kid for cowardice under fire. We always got incoming mortar rounds at night. The mechanic admitted he refused to go out to the flight line. I had never given anyone an Article 15 or a court martial. I didn't blame the kid for being scared, as I have known fear myself. I asked the mechanic if he would go and do his job if I went with him. He agreed to go. I grabbed a rifle and we went out and fixed the Huey by flashlight. I didn't want this soldier to become a different kind of war casualty. I instructed the sergeant to go with his men or at least send someone with them at night.

We need to have a strong military. Today our military would have a hard time fighting a large force. Our men and equipment should be kept here at home in case we do have a major conflict someday. Iran and North Korea are major threats that we can't handle if our forces are spread all over the globe. Iran and North Korea are bound to cause big trouble some day, and they will probably do so at the same time to split up our response. Yes, we need a bigger and stronger military force.

I couldn't believe it when I heard that young men were serving three tours of combat duty by the time they were twenty-five years old. Iraq and Afghanistan are not worthy enough for that many tours of duty. Think of the long term. Soldiers are killed or wounded by the thousands. There will be long-term commitments by our government to care for the soldiers and their families. It will cost a fortune just for combat stress ailments. The people of Iraq and Afghanistan do not care about all our wounded veterans and their sacrifices.

What kind of policies would you have for wars? Would one be to destroy the enemy wherever they are and as quickly as possible? What about reparations? Usually, we end up funding the replacement of infrastructure after the battles are over. Can we afford any more foreign wars?

There are two economic wars today, and our government is not fighting back. One war is with OPEC, and the other war is with China. Both of these entities have been ripping us off for years. We have lost hundreds of billions of dollars to these economic warriors. When will we wake up? The money lost represents American labor for the benefit of foreign countries. I would rather that our labor and innovation benefit our own children and grandchildren.

THE TEA PARTY

The Tea Party has the right ideas: the government is too big; the government spends too much money; the government should not be involved in every little aspect of our lives; and there are too many regulations and programs. These are problems at the state, local, and federal level.

The federal government allows peaceful demonstrations, or in the case of the Wall Street demonstrators, the government allows scumbags to trash our cities. However, the government and the media made fun of the Tea Party and dismissed their concerns because the demonstrations were so peaceful. The Tea Party needs a new strategy. The only way to make these politicians pay attention is to hit them hard where it hurts. You have to punch them in the stomach and disrupt their world. I don't know exactly what to do, but the pocketbook would be one place to hit them. To hit them money-wise we need to do something drastic with their tax revenues at the state and federal level. For example, we could all have $10 per month taken out of our paychecks instead of the $800 a month they now take out. The other $790 a month could go into a savings account and then all of us could send in our taxes on April 12. This action would screw up the government money management for a while.

Instead of the Tea Party having a lot of small meetings and rallies they could hold one giant demonstration in Washington, DC. Yes, the demonstrations should block access to some of those huge government office buildings. The politicians are not going to make things better unless they are forced to do so. I'm sorry; that's the way it is. How about a big airport near DC where everybody could block the runway for a day? I have written congressmen before, and all I get is a form letter that says, "Thanks!" They never respond directly to the issue with any action they are going to take. Nothing changes.

Lately, the Tea Party seems to be associated too closely with the Republican Party. I wish it would have kept a little distance from the Republican Party in order to remain independent. The Tea Party could put more pressure toward conservatism if they kept their distance. Too many Republicans are willing to compromise on taxing and spending. The Tea Party is needed to remind politicians that we want less federal spending and reduced personal taxes. We cannot increase our standard of living with more taxes and more federal spending.

What should the Tea Party do to get action taken? Do you think the Tea Party should distance itself from the Republican Party?

UNITED NATIONS

Why do we need a United Nations and a State Department? The United Nations has outlived its original purpose. The UN was formed in 1942 to employ resources against the Axis powers and not to make a separate peace with the Axis powers like Germany and Japan. The US is a sovereign nation. A sovereign nation has supreme and independent power or authority in government. Recently, the UN has been imposing restrictions on our sovereignty. Why should other countries be able to tell us what to do? What gives us the right to tell other countries what to do or not to do? The UN, if it continues to exist, needs to stay focused on world peace and not any other subject.

The UN wants to dictate domestic issues like global warming. Their charter should be restricted to world peace. North Korea and Pakistan now have nuclear weapons. The UN seems to have failed. Wars keep breaking out all over the world. The UN has failed again.

I would disband the UN and let the State Department deal with international issues. We should determine what is best for the

US without UN interference. Has the UN resulted in a safer or better world? I don't think so!

What do you think? Should we get rid of the UN? The UN likes to spend our US money!

DEFENSE SUPPLY AGENCY

Straight out of college in 1974 I accepted a job with the Defense Supply Agency in Columbus, Ohio. This agency was probably the best I ever worked for. Our mission was to procure supplies and equipment for all the armed services. The rules were simple: buy in quantity common items that were made in the United States. Our activity saved the Department of Defense a lot of money. Naturally, the individual branches of the armed services didn't like us very much. If the air force wanted a hammer they had to get the same hammer the army received. You can guess what happened next: the government eliminated the agency. Later, the horror stories about $200 air force hammers hit the news.

Today the armed services can buy pistols made in foreign countries. Everybody has different pistols and of course they all have different repair parts and ammunition. The old Defense Supply Agency would not have allowed this to happen because it is not cost efficient and the items are not made in the United States.

In Columbus the Defense Construction Supply Center employees were dedicated and they were patriotic. A senior official from Washington came to brief us and he promised he would help us find jobs with other federal agencies. The next day I started sending out résumés and applications. Other employees were surprised, as they were waiting for the return of the senior official. I got lucky and received an offer from HUD in Chicago, so I transferred right away. The senior official found himself a job with DCAA (Defense Contract Audit Agency). That senior official left everyone else hanging out on their own, and he never helped anybody but himself.

One of the reasons we have lost jobs in this country is that the military can buy products and components that are made in foreign countries.

Solution: The government needs to go back to requiring US-made products for the armed services and standardize a lot of supplies and equipment. Millions of dollars a year could be saved, and American small businesses could prosper by supplying the military with items that are now purchased overseas.

Every item the military uses should be made in America.

Your notes and ideas:

HOUSING AND URBAN DEVELOPMENT (HUD)

HUD became a cabinet level agency in 1965. In 2012 the HUD budget was about $48 billion, and in 2013 it is about $56 billion. How big is this budget going to be in five years? You would think that after all these years HUD would be done providing housing for people. Most of the money this agency spends is for rental assistance. Management and administration cost is about $1.6 billion per year.

I have a good plan for this agency. Just eliminate the entire agency. Turn over all the properties to the states or sell them to private investors. The rental assistance money can be turned over to the states. The states have assistance programs of their own, so the taxpayers are paying for two levels of management. The US Treasury can just write fifty-one checks each year.

I worked for HUD in 1978 at the Chicago office. I was a traveling auditor working for the Office of the Inspector General (OIG). The OIG sent me to a lot of low-income neighborhoods in a lot of cities. I remember in particular East St. Louis, Illinois. This city looked like a bombed out WWII disaster. The city government was corrupt. HUD actually relocated residents to other nearby towns. The government bought houses, churches, and businesses and bulldozed them. Everybody was paid relocation expenses. What a mess. The city was not even safe so I had to rent a room across the river in St. Louis, Missouri, and take a bus to work each day. Somebody beat up the city accountant while I was there so that limited my work. I did find that the city had improperly purchased a fire truck with redevelopment grant funds, which was prohibited by the block grant.

The OIG also sent me to audit housing projects in west Chicago and in Peoria. This was a wakeup for a young guy from Iowa. I couldn't believe the filth and squalor that people lived in. Our government was paying for this public housing that was definitely not appreciated by the people living in it. You know what they say about not having any skin in the game? During the day there were not any adults around. Children ran around unsupervised. The kids burned up the elevators by riding up and down in them all day. A lady in one small apartment was doing day care for about twenty kids. Supposedly the adults don't have jobs so where the hell were they? I did something unusual and drove to the project at 11 p.m. Holy cow, there were Buicks and Chevrolets all over the place whereas in the daytime all the parking spaces were empty. This was in Peoria. By 7 a.m. the next morning all the cars were gone. So, here is the scam: you have a good paying job at Caterpillar or someplace and you get your girlfriend pregnant. The girlfriend claims she doesn't know who papa is, so she gets a subsidy for housing and some food stamps. The papa has a good job and buys a new Buick. Papa comes home every night at 10 p.m. while the social workers are sleeping and leaves at 6 a.m. to go get breakfast on his way to work.

After a couple years of seeing dog poop in apartments and filthy bathrooms I gave up and transferred to a different agency. I still remember the burnt up kitchens and clogged up plumbing and feel sorry for those children. Those kids had lazy parents, and they didn't even teach their kids how to keep a house clean. One woman told me it costs money to keep a house clean. I told her a can of Comet or Ajax costs about fifty cents and I could clean two houses for fifty cents.

On another assignment I went to Detroit, Michigan, to do an audit. The government had built a lot of nice little brick homes for low-income people but the people were supposed to pay monthly rent.

Only about half the people paid rent, so a lot of them were evicted. The people evicted would trash the houses. They tore out the plumbing and the carpet and painted graffiti on the walls. One house I inspected had a bomb planted in the living room so I had to call the police.

Patricia Harris was the Secretary of HUD in 1978. One of her pet projects was that she built a highrise apartment building in Chicago for the low-income people. She forgot to ask the people what kind of buildings they preferred. The people didn't want their kids in a high rise so they broke out all the windows before the building was even finished. I think they sold the building to a private investor for less than what it cost to build it.

In Chicago I was offered my first big bribe. Auditing a mismanaged apartment complex the manager offered me a job as a truck driver for the City of Chicago. This guy must have been connected with City Hall. The job offered entailed going to a basement and sleeping all night five days a week in a dorm with a bunch of other guys that never had to drive anything. I declined his offer and wrote my audit report the way it should have been written. The building was poorly maintained with most of the maintenance money going to the manager's pocket. The manager had a unique way of controlling the temperature of the building in the winter. The heat was set at an unbearable eighty-eight degrees and if a cooler temperature was desired the windows were opened and closed as needed. You should have seen the steam. After all, the government paid the heating bills.

I realize that it was 1978 when I had my experiences, but I doubt things have changed much. When the federal government manages programs they do so in a centralized organization and they just don't get out to the grassroots very often. Many times I felt that the top HUD officials really didn't want to know the details. It would be better if HUD programs were handled by small county offices. What good is it to have thousands of people in a big office building in Washington, DC? The HUD employees are too far removed from the activities.

There was one housing project in Illinois that was properly managed. It wasn't managed by a federal employee but by a minister and two prominent businessmen. The units were properly maintained and the people were qualified to live there. Even the grounds were neat and the children were properly behaved. This project was set up as a non-profit corporation. The minister truly cared about people and counseled them on how to have a nice and a safe community.

Shall we get rid of HUD? After more then thirty-five years don't you think HUD should be finished with their job? Is it time for the states and counties to take over?

When you review the budget authority document for HUD (some excerpts are in the appendices), you are just totally overwhelmed. How did so many different programs ever get started? I can only guess that some congressmen got their pet programs passed to get votes for their re-election. Eventually, everybody gets a new program without eliminating any of the old programs. When it is time for re-election they have something to tout to the voters.

Lead paint has not been applied to homes for over forty years but HUD still has a program for it. There is private mortgage insurance available, so why do we need Fannie Mae and Ginne May? Why is there a separate program for Indian Housing? Aren't Indians just citizens like us? A lot of the budget items are so generic you can't tell what they are spending money on.

Scan through appendix six to see all the programs HUD administers.

Please provide your opinion:

HEALTH AND HUMAN SERVICES (HHS)

This agency is just way too big. The two major programs are Medicare and Medicaid. There are lots of smaller programs benefiting tiny segments of the population. Medicare is so large now that it should be a separate agency. HHS has over 76,000 employees for 2013, up from 73,000 in 2011. There is no way anybody can effectively manage an agency this large. I don't really worry about Medicare because revenue from taxpayers and our employers pays for most of the program. They do need to do a better job of controlling the high costs of Medicare. Medicaid is a separate issue, as it is a big welfare program without any offsetting revenue of its own. Also, there is a lot of fraud in this program.

There are ridiculous programs at HHS: Global Health $363 million; medical expenditure surveys $59 million; performance bonuses to states $? millions; enrolling children in Medicaid $40 million; incentives for Medicaid prevention programs $100 million; family violence prevention $139 million; promoting safe and stable families $485 million; and low income energy assistance $2.7 billion. Add all this stuff up and you get 3.9 billion dollars that do not benefit most Americans but only benefit certain groups of people. Can we afford all this?

The HHS budget is just enormous at about $932 billion for 2013. There are some excerpts of their budget in the appendices of this book. I am just scratching the surface here. Their budget documents are too lengthy to include in this book. They are available on the Internet. In one sitting I was trying to read the budget and I became so depressed I had to stop. I was thinking, "My God, who could ever dream up such a massive menu of which 44 percent is just pure welfare crap? I am surprised that they don't have a separate program for the tooth fairy. How can you even distribute $932 billion dollars in one year?"

Just when do we put a reasonable limit on how much a federal agency like this can spend? Remember, the Constitution does not mention that the federal government can just give money away. You know that HHS will ask for more money every year and will find a way to spend every dime they can get. In Minnesota they used to knock on doors and beg people to apply for energy assistance.

Do you think this agency is too big and spends too much?

THE ARMY CORPS OF ENGINEERS

This agency actually accomplishes some extraordinary feats of engineering. Yes, they physically accomplish things that benefit everybody. A lot of the work is done by civilian contractors. You are probably most familiar with the dams and water control activities.

I am relating a story of when I worked for the Corps in St. Paul, Minnesota. The purpose of the story is to show how politics can really add to the cost of some projects. In St. Paul we were primarily involved with dredging the Mississippi River and rebuilding the locks and dams to maintain navigation on the river. We also did flood control projects.

Congress had a program to promote minority businesses. Our office hired a minority contractor named Kathy's Cranes to do a construction project down south on the river. I was assigned to audit the project during construction. First, I went to the site to see if work was being accomplished and it was. I noticed that someone had put tape over the name stenciled on a crane. I removed the tape and found a name other than Kathy's Cranes.

Next, I went to their office in the Twin Cities to audit the records. The accountant acted very strange. He was young and inexperienced and was obviously upset about something. He showed me the file cabinets and said he would be back in two days. I never saw him again. I started going through the records and began finding all sorts of strange information. It turned out that the company didn't own any cranes. This contractor had been approved by the regional Small Business Administration representative. Anyway, the company only had three full-time employees. The owner, a secretary, and the accountant were the only people on the payroll. The company didn't own any equipment and didn't employ any construction workers. I found records that showed the SBA representative had a financial interest in the company. The short of it was that this company was just a storefront operation that leased equipment and hired real contractors to do all the work. The records also showed that contractors had provided special monetary favors to the woman that owned Kathy's cranes. I went to my supervisor and told him I thought that the company was fraudulent. The woman owner had claimed she was Hispanic and in my opinion she just had a good tan and a Texas accent. My boss didn't believe me at first. I finished the audit and recommended that the matter be referred for a criminal investigation. As luck would have it the SBA representative came to our office to complain about my audit and he threatened me in the lobby. My boss overheard the threat and decided I was right about the fraudulent activities. As time went on the FBI ended up doing the investigation. The SBA representative and the owner of Kathy's Cranes were indicted two years later. I testified in court and my work papers proved that there was fraud. They were both convicted.

The main problem with all of this is that these programs not only lend themselves to fraud but that they add a lot of cost to completing a project. You end up paying for two sets of overhead costs and two sets of profit when you do business this way. The army could have hired a legitimate contractor and only paid one level of overhead and one level of profit. You can imagine the cost of the audit, the investigation and the prosecution. Funds recovered in this case would not even pay for the investigation. Kathy's Cranes was barred from doing any more federal projects and the SBA representative lost his job.

Most of my experiences with the Corps of Engineers were positive but every audit my boss and I performed resulted in cost savings. You really can't blame the contractors for trying to pad costs and profit a little but you need to audit them during the project to hold their feet to the fire. We always allowed a reasonable profit margin. When Congress passes these special programs they do not realize that the projects will cost more than they should. These special programs need extra oversight and proactive management.

How do we educate Congress? Send them letters?

FEDERAL EMPLOYEES

If you are employed by the Department of Defense or the military you are required to be sworn in by taking an oath of office. Some of the civilian agencies do not require you to take the oath of office. The oath of office is: "I, NAME, do solemnly swear (or affirm) that I will support and defend the Constitution of the United States against all enemies, foreign and domestic: that I will bear true faith and allegiance to the same; that I take this obligation freely, without any mental reservation or purpose of evasion; and that I will well and faithfully discharge the duties of the office on which I am about to enter. So help me God." All federal employees should be required to take the oath but it is not mandatory in all federal agencies.

From my twenty-seven years of service I have deduced that about half of all federal agency employees are dedicated and they work very hard to discharge their duties. I salute those employees because, as dedicated as they are, it is difficult to overcome the politics that often impede their attempts to complete their work. They often succeed in spite of poor leadership from their supervisors.

Naturally I have a lot of stories about the other half of the federal employees that do not faithfully discharge their duties. Poor leadership contributes to their inefficiency.

I was working on a budget when the National Lab changed the number of nuclear tests they were to conduct about twenty-four hours before the budget was to be submitted. I was really pressed for time. I asked a secretary to help me copy documents and bind them. She stated she was too busy to help. This secretary was always on the phone for personal reasons or she was chitchatting with other workers. I told her it was an emergency and she told me to find someone else to help. I could hardly contain myself, as she was sitting at her empty desk doing nothing. I had to be extremely firm to get her off her butt.

We had an unofficial luncheon one day to celebrate someone's promotion. Somebody told an off-color joke that was overheard by a clerk. The clerk filed a sexual harassment complaint against the joke-teller. This clerk had a temper and often used the "F" word in the office when other employees were around.

The agency required everyone to attend sexual harassment training. In the training it was mentioned that you couldn't put your hand on a woman's shoulder because you might be feeling how deep her bra strap was digging into her shoulder. You were not allowed to compliment women about their personal appearance. There were hundreds of words you were not allowed to speak. One lady complained because I had called her "honey." In Las Vegas it was common for people to use the term "honey" when communicating. I was over fifty years old and when addressing a twenty-year-old young lady I accidentally called her a girl. I got chewed out royally. I soon learned not to talk to any women at work which meant I had to do everything myself.

One employee was doing the annual inventory for cementing materials for the last ten years. I was assigned to review the inventory. I found that the employee didn't keep track of materials issued. He just counted the inventory on hand at the end of each year. You are supposed to take last year's ending inventory and subtract the issuances and add in the new purchases and compare that number to this year's ending inventory. He blew a gasket when I suggested that he was not conducting the inventory properly. If there were losses, nobody would ever know. He did apologize about a year later.

One lady filed a legitimate sexual harassment case against her supervisor. The supervisor just retired early and left the agency. Management was upset that she had filed the case so they decided to punish her by not giving her anything to do. The next three years she wasn't allowed to do any work or attend any meetings. Naturally, she became a disgruntled employee. Previously, she was a good worker and a very intelligent woman. She filed a discrimination case and constantly complained to anyone who would listen to her.

My computer broke down and I had a lot of work that needed to be completed. One of my supervisors was nice enough to let me use his computer because he would be out of the office for a few days. I logged on and saved my work to a file. When I attempted to print out my work the printer wouldn't print anything. I brought up the list of files on the computer to copy my work to a disk. The only files on the computer were the ones I had just created. The supervisor had given me his password but he didn't have any files on his computer. When he returned I told him his printer didn't work. He said, "Oh yes, it hasn't worked for over a year." I guess he didn't need a printer, because he didn't do anything anyway. His office was full of religious books and nothing else. He was always closing his door and doing church-related work at the office because he was a financial counselor for people at his church.

I was assigned to be a team leader for a special project. Various supervisors each assigned one of their employees to be on the team. At our first meeting one member was complaining about how busy she was and that she didn't know how much she would be able to do. I told her that was fine and she could just leave, and that she was dismissed from the team. She became upset and stated that she was supposed to be a team member. I told her that only people willing to do their share would be on my team and repeated that she should leave. I gave all the other team members assignments and deadlines. All the remaining team members buckled down and got their work done on time. The lady I dismissed actually did me a favor because the other members were afraid they would be dismissed.

A lot of federal employees are not properly supervised. Their managers just do not challenge them or give them significant assignments. Eventually, the employees just give up and coast along doing practically nothing. Some employees have a strange philosophy: if you don't do anything you won't make any mistakes so just stay out of trouble and collect your pay. Other employees are happy just receiving paperwork and filing it or sending the paperwork to someone else. They waste their life and don't accomplish anything worthwhile.

One year a contractor came to my office to hook up an answering machine to my phone. I told him I didn't want an answering machine because I answer my phone when it rings. Back then it cost $5 per phone per month to have an answering machine. The secretary that I shared with ten other people had an answering machine and multiple phone lines so I didn't need an answering machine. The other 300 people in our building all got machines. The answering machines heralded a new way of doing business. I witnessed hundreds of times when phones rang and employees didn't answer the phone sitting in front of them. Most often the people could avoid doing work by not returning calls on their answering machines because the person calling would call somebody else to get the work done right away. Sometimes people would comment that they didn't like the caller and that's why they weren't answering the call. So much for caller ID. If the ID means work, you just don't answer the phone.

A young auditor working for HUD in Chicago was assigned a one-week audit in California. After a week he called and asked for an additional week to complete his assignment. He returned to the winter winds in Chicago and claimed that someone had broken into the trunk of his car. The only thing the thief took was all the audit work papers. He had a really nice California tan. I lived with this character and worked with him on other projects. His idea of auditing was to ask the organization being audited for all kinds of data and written procedures. Then, he would put all the papers in a file and conclude that everything was in accordance with federal rules and regulations. He never had an audit finding in his life. After a year he received his first promotion.

There was a person in Nevada that had a full-time position closing contracts. Closing contracts is complicated and takes some serious effort. After a year and a half the managers asked me to help close contracts as there were too many open contracts with funding that needed to be redistributed or closed out. I found out that the contract person had not even closed one contract. The only thing that person had done for over a year was to keep a listing of open contracts. For $45,000 a year, a list was maintained. Somebody could have spent one hour a month to do the same thing. I was able to close three large contracts in three months by working one day a week for the three months. The employee now requested a promotion. The promotion was denied by management. In response, the employee filed a formal complaint that specific training had not been made available. The personnel office found that training classes requested had been denied. Therefore, management was required to promote the person that didn't close any contracts and was required to send the employee to a training class. I closed contracts by reviewing the regulations on my own time at night. You don't need a formal class to close contracts. The employee mentioned was a very lazy person that I had observed for over five years.

There are so many stories I could tell. The problem is with managers and supervisors that are just plain afraid to confront their employees. The supervisors do not review the work being done or hold anyone to any kind of standard. If a manager deems a person to be incompetent the manager just doesn't assign any meaningful work to that person. Management is scared to death that someone will file a complaint against them. Back in Washington, the managers and supervisors stress to the field managers that their appraisals and careers will suffer if even a few personnel complaints are made against them. Supervisors are afraid to keep records on employee performance for fear that they will be sued. The entire environment and the personnel regulations need to be changed. In the meantime the federal employee workforce will just continue to be less efficient and effective.

FEDERAL PERSONNEL MANAGEMENT

Common sense would dictate that you hire the most qualified people and promote the best workers. Forget about common sense in this field. The way it works is you hire and promote based on political considerations. The alleged minorities have a big leg up here. I believe it was Jesse Jackson that preached to people that they should go to work for the federal government because that way they could avoid discrimination. He also preached to them that they then could work from the inside to change things. Well, the real minority soon became the White Anglo Saxon Protestant (WASP). Of course politically, there are not any preference programs for WASPs unless they are veterans.

Let's try to fire a worthless federal employee. This story actually happened. There was a lawyer working for the Dept. of Energy (DOE) in Nevada. I needed to contact the lawyer to get some data for an audit I was working on. I could never find the lawyer and my phone calls were never returned. Finally, I asked the secretary where the hell this lawyer was all the time. The secretary wouldn't say anything until I promised her that nobody would know I interviewed her. She told me that the lawyer hardly ever came to work at all. I found out where the lawyer parked her car and I watched the lot from time to time and kept notes. The lawyer's agenda was to show up about 10 a.m. and go to lunch at noon and then disappear for the rest of the day.

More investigation revealed that the lawyer was improperly getting drugs from a druggist in Florida and was sharing the drugs with the manager of the legal office. Finally, I went to the lawyer's office and went through the files. I didn't find any evidence that the lawyer did any DOE work during the last year. I did find boxes full of documents about saving marine life off the coast of California. All the documents were from a computer legal service paid for by the DOE. I went to management with my information. Management stated that I wasn't authorized to keep an unofficial personnel file on someone. For crying out loud, it was an audit file. I told management I wanted this lawyer fired. Management just about had a heart attack. They didn't know how to fire anyone, let alone a lawyer. Management was also afraid of a lawsuit because, you guessed it: this lawyer was a woman. The woman was an alleged minority due just to being female. I was determined, so I took care of it the only way I knew how. I leaked it to one of the lawyer's friends that I wanted to get her fired. She jumped ship and got a job out east with a different federal agency. Now I had her. When you transfer to a different agency you are on probation for three to six months. When you are on probation you can be fired very easily. I called her new boss and clued him about her work schedule of two hours a day for $70,000 a year. Her new boss didn't believe me, because she had a glowing recommendation from DOE management. I asked him to please watch her for a few weeks. I knew she wouldn't be able to change her bad habits. I called her boss after a month and asked how the lawyer was doing. He said, "Unfortunately, we had to let her go." I felt I did the right thing and was lucky I didn't get sued. Finally, the lawyer was off the federal dole.

You can see how the government ends up with a lot of people doing very little. Managers do not know how to fire anyone and even supervisors are not allowed to keep records on attendance and behavior. The current procedure is to give bad employees good appraisals so they can try to transfer them someplace else.

The current environment is so well-established that I really don't know how the federal government can ever fire anyone. I can only think that to get rid of somebody you need to eliminate their position. If that is done, no one else can be hired to do their job or you risk being sued.

When they give an incompetent worker a good appraisal to try get rid of them they really step into it. The worker might not want to relocate, and the next thing you know the employee wants a promotion. The employee now has a glowing appraisal to show that indeed a promotion is in order. Next thing you know, they are promoting someone that they want to get rid of.

Does anyone out there know how to fire a federal employee? If so, let me know, so I can put it in Volume II.

In my twenty-one years of federal service at five different agencies I cannot remember anyone being fired by agency management. Does that seem a little odd?

FEDERAL AUDITORS

President Clinton and Vice-President Gore didn't like auditors. They claimed that the "auditors were just auditing other auditors." They eliminated a lot of audit positions. The real problem with auditors was that the auditors had to report to their own managers of the agencies to which they were assigned. Therefore, the auditors were not independent. Management would often ignore the audit reports, not issue the reports, or pressure the auditors to tone down the language in the reports. It makes sense the managers would do this, because the managers didn't want to look incompetent, especially if they *were* incompetent. All auditors should report directly to the GAO or to congress. Sometimes, when auditors did contact the GAO, the GAO would just refer the matter right back to the agency concerned, and direct management to investigate further. The GAO should not do that.

In my opinion all audit reports should go to congress and auditors should not be supervised by the agency they are auditing. We need a congressional committee to review all audit reports and the committee should ensure corrective action is taken by the various agencies.

Another problem with audits is that they are seldom proactive. Most audits are accomplished after the year is over or the project is completed. Most audits should be done during the current year or during the project work so problems can be corrected before all the money has been wasted. If you do audits a year or two later you have already wasted money that cannot be recovered.

One stupid idea the government had was to have contractors hire their own internal auditors. There isn't any independence in that situation and if you read their reports they usually state that everything is hunky-dory. These auditors are paid with federal funds but they are not looking out for the taxpayer's interests.

Many of the auditors I knew would interview managers, review written procedures, and look at the regulations. Then, they would conclude that everything was in compliance and write a nice, clean audit report. Managers and supervisors loved these auditors because they could bullshit their way to a clean slate. I had a totally different approach. I insisted on beginning my audits with a visit to the actual worksite where I looked at the work being done, and I interviewed the front-line workers. Then, I did what the other auditors did. Finally, I would compare the actual field operations with the other information. I usually found out that the work was being done differently than the written procedures and totally differently from what the managers thought was happening. The cause of this is that the managers are too lazy to go to the field, or they get too busy going to a bunch of useless meetings.

The hardest part of auditing is identifying the root cause of problems. If you don't identify the root cause and an adverse effect, you don't really have an audit finding. Whoever started the TV show *Undercover Boss* must have been a good auditor at one time, because that show is a prime example of what is wrong with some businesses and most government operations: management is too far removed from the worksite and the workers.

Maybe what we need is a *Reader's Digest* of all audit reports. The media mentions GAO reports once in a blue moon but usually doesn't provide any details. There are hundreds of audit reports that never come to the attention of the public. GAO is not the only audit organization. Most agencies have internal auditors and inspector generals that issue reports. The public has a right to know which agencies are doing a good job and which ones are not.

What are your thoughts? Do we need more auditors and more public disclosure of the audit reports?

THE DEPARTMENT OF EDUCATION

The most powerful force in our high schools is peer pressure. To improve education this force needs to be applied in the right direction. Our educators do not know how to motivate their students. Discipline and hard work have fallen by the wayside as technology has diverted attention away from core values. Perhaps we should select a few special students and have them motivate their peers. The school curriculums could also be revised to emphasize vocational training as well as the basic classes in the three Rs.

For some reason parents are not as involved with their kids' education as they are in providing a cell phone, 200 TV channels, and video games for their kids. You can't leave it up to the counselors or the kids to pick the right classes. Many kids will pick a lot of easy classes or physical education classes just to get enough credits to graduate on time. One way I motivated my children was in order to get a drivers license they had to have a B average. Their grades immediately went from a C to a B.

I have attended several high school graduations and I couldn't believe it when they announced the scholarships given. Over half the graduates received a scholarship but they were only for $100 to $200. It didn't seem to matter if you had good grades, excellent grades, or poor grades. Everybody received $100 or $200. College books are over $100 each. Where are the real grants of $1000 or more? Some A-average students didn't even receive a grant. Where is the incentive to be an A-average student? We definitely need a change of venue. The country spends billions of dollars without any benefit to its citizens. Let us reprogram some of those funds and provide free tuition for one year to our A and B average students to attend college or some other training program. Then, the high school graduates can prepare themselves for jobs that are available. If the students want to attend longer than one year then they or their families can take care of the continuation of their training. The government is too focused on low-income families and most grants go to that cause. There are too many middle-class students that must struggle to pay for schooling. The emphasis should be on students with good grades in school, and all the students regardless of financial status will soon learn to buckle down and do better in high school.

A big deterrent to getting a good high school education is that the students do not spend enough time in classes. The school day should be extended by an hour or more to include a thirty minute study hall. A lot of high school students only go to classes four or five hours a day.

I believe that the only role of the federal government in education is to provide funding. The funding should be distributed based on the population of each state. Failing schools should not get additional funding because they are not performing well. The US Department of Education should be eliminated. The Treasury Department can distribute funding to states. State and local governments and the PTA can take care of the public schools and the charter schools without federal interference.

The Department of Education budget document is amazing. There are excerpts of the budget in Appendix I. If you read through the budget you will notice that the worst schools in the nation get the most money. That's right, the more incompetent your teachers and administrators are, the more money the school gets. This is some incentive for the educators. There are even provisions for the lousy teachers to get free training and a new title so they can make more salary. Something tells me that you are not supposed to reward failure. Maybe I am screwy, but I thought you were supposed to reward the people that are doing a great job above expectations.

Somehow I was able to get a decent education in the 1960s without the federal government sending millions of dollars to the State of Iowa. All we had was a piece of free land, which required the boys to take ROTC (Reserve Officer Training Corps) in high school. We didn't have a pool and we didn't have air conditioning but we had long hours and a mandatory study hall.

Every year they increase my property taxes to improve education. This state money is supposed to pay for K-12 education. Why do states need all that federal money?

You will notice that the top people in the Department of Education are big Obama supporters as they brag him up in their budget narrative. Of course President Obama has given this agency extra millions to spend on all kinds of crazy initiatives. Please read through some of the narrative in Appendix I to see just how goofy some of the new initiatives are.

Pell grants are given to low-income undergraduate students. They can receive up to $5,550 per year. Pell grants are not loans, so the student does not have to pay back the money and does not pay any interest on the money they receive. If you are from a middle-class family you cannot qualify for a Pell grant no matter how good your grades are. The middle class student must get loans and often must pay 6 percent interest on some of the loans while they are in school. Where does the Pell grant money come from? It doesn't come from low-income families because they don't pay federal taxes. The government needs to get rid of the income qualification. For example, if I am twenty years old and in college it shouldn't matter how much my parents' income is. What matters is what my personal income is. Parents are really not responsible to pay for college costs for their children that are over the age of eighteen. So, why is the parents' income a factor in whom gets grants?

You decide—should the Department of Education be eliminated? Your comments:

SOCIAL SECURITY

Wasn't it nice of the government to design social security with a retirement age of sixty-five and expect you to die at age sixty-seven? Wasn't it nice that they took your money and the money your employer paid in and then spent the money on other government programs? You think that maybe all that money should have been put in an interest-bearing bank account? Isn't it nice that you get about $1500 per month pension instead of about $2000 per month? That's right, if you had been in a state program that was exempt from social security and earned the same amount, you would get $2000 per month instead of $1500 per month. In Minnesota if you work for a city, they deduct social security and state retirement payments from your check. If you work for a city in Nevada they only take the state pension payment out of your check. Why isn't it the same for every state? I don't know.

Our current politicians are a bunch of real screwballs. They changed the retirement age to sixty-seven. They make us worry about the future of our benefits and it's our fault because we haven't died soon enough. You would think maybe it is the fault of past politicians that mismanaged the program. Depending on your occupation it is nearly impossible to work full time at age sixty-six. We are worn out at age sixty-five. Are you going to be able to lay carpet, do roofing, or safely drive a semi truck at age sixty-seven? I can think of hundreds of jobs you cannot physically do at age sixty-seven.

What about a government pension offset? The offset is about 45 percent of your social security. This little tweak to social security was supposed to save social security a lot of money by cheating people out of nearly half their social security. What a lousy reward for people that worked hard at a lot of different jobs. So, you keep working and then they tax your social security. Between the tax and the offset you lose over 50 percent of your social security. This is a double whammy! You are even paying tax on money you paid tax on years ago. Talk about immoral and nasty! This takes the cake, or should I say, the government gets the cake and you get the crumbs.

Can anybody live on $1500 a month anymore? My grandmother had to sell her home when she went on social security. Some security, her home was paid for but taxes and upkeep were too expensive. Her husband died at age sixty-six after collecting social security for about six months. Because Grandma qualified for her own social security of about $800 a month she didn't get any benefits from Grandpa working for thirty-six years.

The government needs to pay back the social security fund and put all social security money in an interest-bearing account. They should pay a penalty because they basically stole our money. Repeal the offset and set the retirement age at sixty-four, not sixty-seven. Also, forget about taxing anybody's social security regardless of how much they make. We paid taxes over the years on all the money we paid into social security. Remember, the government stole our retirement money and spent it on God knows what so the government is responsible to make things right.

The survivor benefit section of social security is just another welfare program, so fund it under a welfare program and do not fund it from social security. I knew a lady that was divorced with two sons. Her ex-husband killed himself when the boys were about nine years old. She received social security for the two boys until they were twenty years old. The fact that she made good money working for the Post Office didn't matter. The fact she remarried and her husband made $70, 000 a year didn't matter. The payments from social security just kept coming. If there were to be government assistance it should not have come from the social security funds. Their combined income of $120,000 per year was adequate to raise two boys.

Guess what the retirement age is for federal employees that were under CSRS?

Answer: Civil Service Retirement System (CSRS) retirement is age fifty-five with full-earned benefits.

Give me your point of view on social security: Do you have any stories to tell about your family?

OVER AND OVER AGAIN

Is it time for a tax revolt? It doesn't matter how you think politically when it comes to the question of taxes in general. We all pay too much! In fact, we are being robbed blind.

If I give someone a gratuity/tip they must pay taxes on their tips. I already paid taxes on that money. If I buy hunting and fishing equipment a tax is built into the price and then I pay sales tax on top of a tax. This applies to many other items, like alcohol.

If you gamble and win more than $1500 you have to pay taxes on your winnings. That money came from other people that gambled and lost money that they had already paid taxes on. So, the same dollar gets taxed twice. Some gambling wins have been labeled as prizes so you are not allowed to deduct your losses. If you don't itemize deductions you cannot write off your gambling losses against your winnings. Senior citizens get clobbered here.

In Minnesota I remember the politicians wanted more revenue to blow so they started things like scratch off tickets, lotteries and state run casinos. To get voter support they promised that this would preclude raising other taxes. As time went on they kept raising property and sales taxes anyway. Now there is even sales tax on some services. There is no limit to the amount of money politicians will spend and no limit on the number of lies they will tell.

There are taxes on nearly everything we touch today. Some experts say that the middle-class employees only get to spend about 55 percent of what they earn as the other 45 percent goes for all kinds of hidden taxes, fees, federal income taxes and state income taxes. How are we supposed to save any money for retirement?

In the Declaration of Independence it states that whenever any form of government becomes destructive to our inalienable rights the people have a right to alter or abolish that form of government. I do not advocate any form of government other than that of a republic. We the people do need to alter our government, as it has evolved in ways that were never intended by the founding fathers. As in the book *Atlas Shrugged*, we cannot tolerate a government that intercedes in every aspect of our personal lives and one that tries to control all forms of business enterprise. The taxing of everything ends up affecting every decision we make and therefore controls our behavior.

I can only imagine one way to put a stop to the tax abuse. We need to drastically reduce the size and influence of the government. Several federal agencies and some state agencies need to be obliterated. In this book I suggest huge reductions in agencies like HUD, HHS and the Department of Education. Smaller reductions should be made to the EPA, DOE, Commerce, and State Departments. Just think of all the rules and regulations that could be eliminated. Think about the reduction in taxes that could be achieved. I don't know about you but I would like to have control of 80 percent of what I earn, not 55 percent.

Please send me your thoughts for Volume II.

US DEPARTMENT OF STATE

There is a lot of talk on TV about whose fault it was that our people in Libya were killed. I have the answer. It is the President's fault for even having an embassy in Libya in the first place. Libya just had a revolution and their government was in transition. What the hell were we doing even having a presence there at that time?

The Department of State has over 48,000 employees spread all over the world. There is no way we can protect all of these embassies. Half the embassies are in countries where the government is not friendly to us or countries that don't have the means to protect foreign embassies. There is an obvious answer. Close half of our embassies and bring the people home. If foreign countries need to coordinate trade with us they can send their people over here to the US or they can use either the phone or the computer to coordinate trade.

Closing half the embassies would protect our State Department employees and save about $10 billion a year. Mark my words: another embassy or two will be attacked by somebody very soon, because there are so many radical maniacs running around the world. It is time to minimize risk.

Of the 48,000 employees about 30,000 of them are Foreign Service national employees. This means that we are paying a lot of people that are not even US citizens. Part of the money this agency spent ($1.8 billion) went for providing humanitarian assistance. There they go again: another welfare program. You won't believe this one. They spent $2.7 billion for promoting international understanding. What is that? What do you do under that category? Do you teach people English?

So, what do you think?

US DEPARTMENT OF ENERGY

If you thought that the Department of Energy (DOE) was involved with providing more energy and cheaper energy you would only be 99 percent wrong. Of the stimulus money for fiscal year 2009 and fiscal year 2010 DOE received $38 billion. I haven't heard of any new power plants or new refineries that were built with that $38 billion. The DOE spends very little effort on domestic energy resources. The effort they apply is to reduce or slow down the use of domestic energy and slow down the development of new fossil fuel energy sources. Their effort costs you money because they restrict supply.

The DOE 2013 budget states that to cut wasteful spending and improve efficiency they are going to repeal $4 billion a year in tax subsidies to oil, gas and other fossil fuel producers. This action will increase the prices and restrict supply. What a way to characterize development of fossil fuels. The DOE is willing to spend more than $4 billion on getting energy directly from the sun. For $4 billion I'll bet they get about $1 million worth of energy from the sun. Maybe DOE should relocate its offices to the moon where they can heat the buildings with sunrays.

The DOE is involved with a lot of programs related to national defense and nuclear issues. These other programs are where they place most of their effort. I was lucky enough to be invited to Lawrence Livermore National Lab for a financial meeting. This was years ago. Surprise, in walked the famous Dr. Teller accompanied by his butler of sorts. The butler had an advanced degree in physics. The butler's job was to record everything that Dr. Teller said all the time. I was in awe of Dr. Teller. As he spoke the room became eerily quiet. I didn't understand about 80 percent of what Dr. Teller said, but I understood that he was going to see President Reagan to tell the President that Star Wars would bankrupt the nation. Here was one man that could stop a huge government program in the blink of an eye. Where are such men today? A few weeks later we were officially notified that the Star Wars program was discontinued. Sadly, Dr. Teller is no longer with us. One man made a decision. It wasn't a government agency that called off the program. If it were up to a government agency the program, though not feasible, would still be carried on today.

In 1973 there was an oil crisis. In 1977 the DOE was created. You would think that the main focus of this department would be oil and domestic energy as the Federal Energy Administration, the Energy Research and Development Administration and the Federal Power Administration were folded into the DOE. Somehow, over time, this department lost its focus. Perhaps this agency should be split up again.

The DOE annual budget is about $30 billion a year. The agency is also given other money to hand out and the agency provides loan guarantees to energy companies. The agency lacks the talent to decide what companies should get loans. Remember Solyrindra and battery companies that went broke. The only reason DOE is in the loan business is that the head of the agency is willing to do whatever the President tells him to do. It doesn't matter if it is legal or moral; the agency just does what they are told to do.

The DOE should report directly to congress and take its direction from congress and the law. Also, the agency needs to change its objectives and strive to develop all energy sources that are efficient and cost effective.

If somebody knows how AMOCO became BP I wish they would let me know. American interests were sold down the river on this deal. Maybe we should boycott all BP gas stations until AMOCO re-arises as an American company. Where was the government when this deal came along?

I did a fuel distribution audit in Florida. Fuel is loaded in barges in Louisiana and towed over the Gulf of Mexico to Florida. The barges pump the JP4 (jet fuel) into a pipeline and most of the fuel goes to the navy. Some of the fuel is stored in huge tanks. Guess what? The barges leak fuel. Water gets in the storage tanks. You are lucky if 80 percent of the fuel ever makes it into an aircraft. Does anyone care about the 20 percent that is wasted? No, they don't do anything to reduce losses. Yet, the government is willing to spend billions on wind energy and solar energy. Maybe the government should just spend a few million on preventing waste.

I read somewhere last week that three coal-fired electrical energy plants were being closed down due to government interference. There go more jobs. China burns dirty coal in dirty power plants so closing some of our cleaner burning plants is not going to help the alleged global warming situation. The earth is capable of cleaning the air. Look what happens when a volcano erupts. The volcanic ash and smoke eventually become fertile soil capable of producing food for people.

At the Nevada test site they wanted to build a hangar for helicopters they didn't have. I did an audit and concluded that the agency would probably never get the new choppers. Even if they did get the bigger choppers they would fit into an existing hangar at the test site. About $1 million was programmed for the hangar. I suggested that they cancel the hangar project. Management went nuts on me and insisted on wasting the money. I threatened management by stating I would refer the matter to the General Accounting Office and Congress. I screwed myself but the hangar was never built. The DOE never did, to my knowledge, get the bigger helicopters.

Do you think that the DOE should be split up and report directly to congress?

US DEPARTMENT OF COMMERCE

This department budget (in brief) is 150 pages long. Brief must have a different meaning to the department than what is in the dictionary. In 2011 the budget authority was $5.8 billion, but for 2013 it is estimated to be $9.2 billion. That is a difference of $3.4 billion. If you look at the budget you see two huge additions to the budget. One addition is called NTIA, Public Broadband Network of $1.2 billion and the other is called NIST or National Network for Manufacturing Innovation. On other pages of the budget it looks like $1.2 billion of the above $2.2 billion is taken out or moved elsewhere. So, I'm not sure what is going on, but I do know that with the huge national debt we have that it is not a good time to give this department more money than it had in 2011. This paragraph is confusing because the agency apparently doesn't know what they are going to do with the funding they are requesting.

In 2011 the department had 41,558 people (full-time equivalent, or FTEs) and in 2013 they are going to have 42, 829 FTEs. So much for the government trying to save money. In the budget they take credit for cost savings. Are you kidding me? In 2013 they intend to spend $3.4 billion more than in 2011 so how can they talk about cost savings?

Is this another agency that is 25 percent bigger than it should be? I say that their budget for 2013 should be cut by $4 billion and let the poor souls get by with $5.2 billion.

Somebody help us. We need a whistleblower. What do you think?

Do you even know what this agency does? I know they do the census and allegedly help develop businesses. There are some excerpts of their budget in the appendices that show what they do. They are involved with communications, patents and trademarks.

THE INTERNAL REVENUE
SERVICE (IRS)

The IRS employs over 100,000 employees. The IRS processed over 175 million returns in 2010 and collected $2.3 trillion dollars. The top 5 percent of earners paid 38.3 percent of the taxes collected. Lost tax income in 2001 was estimated to be over $323 billion. I guess not everyone pays their fair share. President Nixon was a beauty. Nixon made $200,000 in 1970 and only paid $793 in federal income taxes. Nixon deducted $571,000 over a few years for donating vice-presidential papers.

In 2009 the IRS budget was 11.5 billion. If we went to a flat tax we could cut the IRS budget down to about 5 billion a year. I'll bet you paid more tax than President Nixon ever did. I think I'll donate this book to the government and just not pay any taxes any more. What can you donate?

I had a friend that worked for the IRS as an agent. He had stories you would not believe. A doctor bought a $100,000 sailboat and deducted $30,000 a year as he claimed the boat was available for lease and was therefore a business. The problem was he only leased it once to a fellow doctor. My friend disallowed the deductions of about $60,000 for two years. Well, the doctor said he was going to go to court, so administratively the IRS supervisors allowed most of the deductions to avoid going to court. Why bother to do an audit if you are going to bend over and allow such a silly deduction? This is the same as having the rest of the honest taxpayers buy the poor doctor a sailboat.

We could save $6 billion a year right here if we had a flat tax and simple forms and instructions. There wouldn't be a bunch of loopholes anymore, and tax revenues would probably go up by $500 million a year as rich people wouldn't have all those big deductions anymore. Some wealthy people have two mansions and get to deduct the interest and property taxes on two homes. They also need to reduce loopholes for businesses. The depletion allowance would be a good loophole to eliminate.

So, put down your thoughts:

THE BUDGET PROCESS

The budget process is complicated, so I will just mention some of the basics. All the federal agencies submit an annual budget request. The congress may or may not pass their budgets. Budget requests are always estimates. It is important to remember that the requests are estimates and that the agencies always inflate their requests. All the agencies are competing with one another to get the most budget authority they can get.

Some agencies have one-year budget authority and some can carry forward budget authority for up to five years. If you have one-year authority you usually need to cheat on your accounting for the money to show that all the money has been committed. It is easy to cheat. You can leave contracts open to show that money is committed or obligated. You can order a bunch of supplies and equipment near yearend to show obligations. At the beginning of the next year you can just cancel some orders or close some contracts to free up additional funds that you improperly carried over to a subsequent year. Figures don't lie but liars figure.

Because budgets are estimates, agencies can revise their budgets during the year. Agencies can reprogram funds. Sometimes when they reprogram funds they spend the money differently than what they originally told congress they were going to do. Now here is the kicker. At the end of the year the agencies show their costs compared to the revised budget. In most cases people never look at the original budget compared to what the money was actually spent on.

Because budgets are estimates and are revised it is really difficult for anyone to really analyze the financial statements. Also, the agencies are so big there just isn't time to analyze everything.

Another difficulty is that cost reports are complicated with thousands of cost codes. To see what money was spent on is a labor-intensive task. A cost can be recorded and coded as outreach to seniors when the cost was really money spent on motel rooms and airline tickets to some useless conference in Las Vegas.

The government needs to revise the cost reports and the budget process. It is ridiculous that it takes hundreds of hours to determine what the money spent actually bought. Oh yes, another trick the agencies use is to have contractors pay for things. The agency can show a support contract cost of $5000 when in actuality some administrator bought a $5000 desk for his office.

In another section of this book I discuss auditing; we need more independent audits.

So, how do you like the budget process?

PATH TO GREATNESS

By now you should be thinking like a president. Today you are the president. So, you might as well become a great one.

World peace: If you could bring peace to earth you would be a great president. There are only a few countries standing in your way. Iran, Syria, North Korea and Pakistan are at the top of the list. Their governments do not want peace on earth. They are basically warring tribes that think the way to a better life is to take from others instead of creating their own wealth.

Energy self-sufficiency: Build power plants, drill for oil and gas, and refine natural resources in the United Sates and elsewhere. Provide cheap and plentiful energy.

Eliminate the national debt: Do not mortgage our future by borrowing money from other countries.

Protectionism: Do not let foreigners own our land and other assets. Put more assets in the hands of US citizens.

Foreign aid: Stop giving away money and military equipment. Instead, help other countries become self-sufficient. Give them tractors and seeds. Give them water treatment equipment. Give them medicine.

Standard of living: Create jobs in the private sector that pays enough to improve the worker's standard of living. Train people to qualify for good jobs. Get that unemployment rate down to about 4 percent nationwide.

Give me some input for Volume II:

IMMIGRATION

Our government is having a big debate over the issue of immigration reform. Again, they are totally going the wrong direction. Immigration is a big problem because the Mexican government will not take the right steps to improve the standard of living of the Mexican citizens. Our government needs to help Mexico develop its natural resources. Mexico can build its own infrastructure without stealing our factories. Mexico needs to work on the sewage systems and clean water systems. Mexico needs to provide better paying jobs for its people.

Building fences and increasing border patrol does not address the root cause of the problem. The problem is the Mexican economy and their low standard of living.

Illegal immigrants should be sent back to their home countries. If the illegal people are caught a second time they should be black-listed from ever applying for a legal status. It is not fair to the people that apply for legal status to let the illegal people stay here. We must have quotas to maintain a balance between jobs available and the flow of workers. Our children need jobs too!

Some countries will not let Americans have jobs in their countries because they have high rates of unemployment. Other countries will not let Americans move there unless the Americans have obtained a job first or they can demonstrate they have enough money to survive there without a job. Here we are debating whether to allow illegal aliens to stay here. I don't care how long the illegal people have been here; they need to go away and apply for a visa legally.

Spending a lot of money on fences is really stupid. There are electronic devices that will show if people are crossing the border. Fences are for cattle, not people. Is there a fence that you could not compromise in about two minutes? Who will maintain the fences? A border fence is as stupid as all those big sound walls they build along the highways. Future maintenance of such silly structures will suck us dry. All those materials could have been used to build homes or businesses. I can't wait to see all those floating fences they will need to build on the Canadian border. Well, maybe the Canadian border needs a thirty-foot high electric fence or a fifty-foot high cement wall topped with razor wire.

Do you think immigration reform is on the right track?

THE ECONOMIC WAR

The first step in fighting the economic war is to identify the enemies and inform the public that we are being attacked. The politicians do not want to take this first step.

The enemies are OPEC, China, and the United Arab Emirates. The countries that have attacked us are: China, Iran, Iraq, Kuwait, Dubai (a city), Libya, Nigeria, Angola, Ecuador, Qatar, Saudi Arabia, Venezuela and Algeria. Their weapons of choice are oil and cheap labor.

Some of the countries above are supposed to be our allies and friends. We don't need friends like these. Other countries are definitely our enemies. Our military protects many of these countries. They are all economic enemies.

In the 1990s a barrel of oil was selling for $15 to $20 a barrel. Today the price jumps all over at about $90 a barrel. The price is often set by political considerations. In the past, the price was increased just because the US supported Israel.

Saudi Arabia is a country of 26.5 million people. The country produces 9.8 million barrels of oil a day. Multiply 9.8 million by $90 a barrel and you are talking about serious money. Saudi Arabia has 17 percent of the world oil reserves. Oil accounts for 45 percent of their GDP. The country experienced 7.1 percent growth in 2011. The government has a surplus of cash every year. Do we have a surplus? It is amazing that they have 26.5 million people but only have a labor force of 8 million people.

Iran produces 3.7 million barrels of oil a day. Kuwait produces 2.5 million barrels of oil a day. The United Arab Emirates produce 2.5 million barrels of oil a day.

Dubai is a city of 2.1 million people. This city has used the oil revenue to diversify the economy. Revenue now comes from tourism, real estate and financial services. Oil production is 70,000 barrels a day and they also sell natural gas. Exports to the US are 5.8 billion dollars a year. Dubai was the 33rd richest city in the world in 2009.

Kuwait has GDP of $43,800 per person. The population is only 2.6 million. The growth rate in 2011 was more than 8 percent. What was the growth rate for the US in 2011? Petroleum accounts for 95 percent of the government revenue and 95 percent of export revenues. The labor force is more than 2 million, but half the labor force is foreigners. Unemployment is only 2 percent. What is the unemployment rate in the US? Kuwait has an economic development plan to spend over $130 billion in a five-year period to diversify the economy. Considering the population of only 2.6

million, $130 billion is a lot of money. Kuwait has a surplus of cash every year.

Our economic enemies have been waging the economic war since 1995, and they have been winning because we are not fighting back. Hundreds of billions of US dollars have left our country to expand the economy of our enemies. We can't get the money back, but we can stop them from getting any more of our money. I will never understand how the interests of countries like Saudi Arabia can be more important than the interests of the American people. Our foreign policies have been a nightmare for the last twenty years and we have a $16 trillion debt to prove it.

Do you think it is time to fight back?

MAINSPRING

The book *Mainspring* was written by Henry Weaver in about 1947. The book was based on the general theme of Rose Wilder Lane's book *The Discovery of Freedom*. The subtitle of *Mainspring* is, "the story of human progress and how *not* to prevent it." I am including some quotes from *Mainspring* because the book is not readily available anymore. The quotes follow:

"We, in these United States of America, have made more effective use of our human energies than any other people on the face of the globe."

"Individual freedom is the natural heritage of each living person."

"Freedom cannot be separated from responsibility."

"A thing is not property unless it is owned, and without ownership there is little incentive to improve it." " In this great country we are able to own land and other productive assets without fear that the government will nationalize our property."

"It is only when men are free that they begin to place a value on their time—and when men begin to place a value on human time they begin to realize the importance of preserving human life."

"The big point is that our progress to date is the result of an entirely new and different form of political structure that has made it possible for human energy and individual initiative to work under their own natural control."

"In America, to a greater degree than in any other country, there has been the opportunity for self-expression, self-development and advancement on the basis of merit—regardless of race, creed, or class distinction."

"In the static world of the pagans, the only way to gain a benefit was to take something away from someone else. Under that philosophy, human energy that might have been used to increase wealth has always been wasted in fighting over existing wealth."

"The matter of taking advantage of the opportunities is up to the individual—and it cannot be otherwise."

"There are no substitutes for self-faith, self-reliance, self-development, individual effort and personal responsibility."

"Life on this earth is no bed of roses. The end of man is not self-indulgence—but achievement. There are no short-cuts, and no substitutes for *work*."

"Military strength rests on a foundation of economic strength."

"Economic strength depends on the number of people who are engaged in productive work—as against the number being supported on public payrolls."

I strongly believe that we need to reduce the number of public workers. Just look at the appendices to see how many federal employees there are in some of the federal agencies. Then, add in some state and county workers, and it is easy to see why the economic strength of our nation has declined so significantly the last ten years.

"Free individuals have greater initiative."

"Free individuals have more to fight for and do not need to be egged on by spurious propaganda." This statement is really applicable to today's world where Islamic extremists use propaganda to rile up their population.

Imagine, all the above was written in 1947. Are we teaching these principles to our children today?

SUMMARY

This book is about the application of human energy. Man's material progress depends on natural resources plus human energy multiplied by tools. The American Economic Foundation came up with this theory way back in the 1940s. What does not fit in this theory is the interference of government. Thousands of federal employees pushing paper to enforce thousands of regulations are counterproductive. We must apply most of our human energy to resources to produce goods for trade and consumption.

In this book I have identified over $400 billion of savings per year. In just four years that would be $1.6 trillion. I realize that the reductions seem pretty drastic but when you realize that all the cuts relate to programs that are counterproductive, the cuts are not drastic at all. When politicians talk about saving $85 billion or talk about some savings over a ten-year period I totally lose interest in what they are talking about. During their ten years I know things will change and the savings will never be achieved. The $85 billion they talk about is just insignificant because it is a reduction of increases in spending. Remember, they estimate the national debt is over $16 trillion.

I look at the budget for the EPA and see that in 1975 the EPA budget was about $700 million. Back in 1975 they had 10,438 employees. Today the EPA budget is $8.4 billion and they have 17,300 employees. What the hell are politicians thinking? It all seems hopeless at times. You can't improve the economic climate by cutting 4 percent of an agency like the EPA. You need to cut 50 percent of the EPA budget and 50 percent of their employees. In fiscal year 1986 the EPA budget was $3.6 billion and that should be their budget for fiscal year 2013.

I wish everybody would read the book *Mainspring: The story of human progress and how not to prevent it*. This book gave us a good warning in 1947 but evidently no one heeded its message. You can make a difference by sending me your ideas on how to save America. I will publish your ideas in Volume II and send it to all the members of the Senate, even if I have to self-publish it and pay for it myself.

In the last four years most of us saw our savings dwindle to half. We didn't do anything foolish except maintain the standard of living we were lucky enough to have achieved. I grieve for all the people that lost their homes. What happened to your personal wealth over the past five years? What about your future and your retirement plans? What about the future of your children? Will your children be able to own a home or own productive assets? Maybe in ten years all the American assets will be in the hands of the OPEC nations, or China will own all our assets. We must take steps now to protect American assets from foreign control and foreign ownership. If we do not protect our assets we will not be able to apply our human energy to resources anymore because we will not own the land and the resources of the land. All could be lost.

Under "increasing revenue," different ways the government could bring in more revenue were identified. Revenue can be increased without increasing taxes on individuals and businesses. I estimate that revenue could increase by $250 billion per year which, over four years, would be $1 trillion. If you add that $1 trillion to cost savings identified in this book you could reduce the debt by $2.6 trillion in just four years. There would be even more savings as our interest payments would also be reduced.

The whole truth and nothing but the truth seems to elude our politicians. Unemployment is reported at 7.3 percent when it is really over 14 percent. They don't report people that have given up looking for work. Inflation is reported at 2.5 percent when for the middle class it is really 5 percent. Inflation is underreported because they don't consider the increase in food and energy prices. The one I really love is when a federal agency reports cost savings when they actually spent more money this year then they did last year. Politicians treat us like we are ignorant sheep. Of course the politicians want to be reelected, so they tell their little white lies until they are blue in the face. The little lies over many years have finally caught up to them, as we are now over $16 trillion in debt.

Now, you are president, so what are you going to do? Will you do what is right for all the people all the time? If some program doesn't benefit all the people, then the federal government should not be involved. Let the individual states worry about specific groups of the population. If people don't like the programs of one state, they can move to a different state. Whenever the federal government passes legislation favoring a special interest group, the rights of the rest of the people are reduced.

When the federal government passes money to states, like for education, the basis for the payments should be the population of the states. When they give extra money to a state with a poor education system it takes away from the states that are doing a good job. Often the alleged power of a prominent senator decides where the most money goes. People only have power if you let them have it. The real power should rest in the hands of the people. When people abuse their positions in the government, they should be removed from office immediately. If all the money the federal people distribute was done on the basis of population, the distribution would be fair to all the states and therefore fair to all the people. Let the states decide which projects and programs receive funding. This type of wealth distribution would reduce the influence and power of the federal government.

We desperately need a truly great president. A great president needs a great mission statement. Statements like: Increase gross national product by 20 percent over four years. Increase the standard of living for all Americans by 16 percent over four years. Provide productive employment for all citizens able to work. Educate every American to achieve his or her full potential.

You are president, so send your mission statement for Volume II. We need some great mission statements for our next president and the Congress. Let's keep America the greatest nation that has ever been on earth.

APPENDIX I:
US DEPARTMENT OF ENERGY

Responsibilities: nuclear weapons program; nuclear reactor production; energy conservation; energy research; radioactive waste disposal; domestic energy production; and Human Genome Project.

Annual Budget: 2012: $30.6 billion

Employees: 16,000 federal and 93,000 contract employees

Nineteen major legislative acts

Total Outlays: 2011: $32.7 billion; 2012: $40.6 billion; 2013: $34.9 billion (estimated).

In 2012 loans of $27.6 billion were disbursed for advanced technology vehicles manufacturing. These funds are in addition to the $40.6 billion spent on the agency's mission.

This agency has lost its focus. They didn't build any new nuclear power plants. Nuclear waste has not been properly disposed of;

it has just been kept in storage. I assume that Hanford is waiting for a major disaster at the Columbia River facility as their nuclear waste has been sitting there for twenty years. The agency has not promoted domestic energy production. Coalmines have been shut down and federal land in Alaska has not been developed for oil production. Also, where are the new refineries?

APPENDIX II:
ENVIRONMENTAL
PROTECTION AGENCY

Responsibilities: protecting human health and the environment; environmental research assessment and education; and pollution prevention programs.

Annual Budget: 1986: $3.6 billion; 1996: $6.5 billion; 2012: $8.4 billion.

Employees: 17,000

Legislation: ten air acts; eleven water acts; eleven land acts; five endangered species acts; and nine hazardous waste acts.

Programs: endangered species; research vessel; greenhouse gases; energy star; pesticide; environmental impact statements; safer detergents; fuel economy; air quality; oil pollution; water sense; drinking water; and radiation protection.

The EPA and DOE obviously have some duplicate responsibilities. Back in 1977 this agency's budget was only $2.7 billion but today has grown to $8.4 billion. It might be time to repeal a few of the forty-six acts and cut the budget down a few billion. This agency makes it difficult and expensive to open a new factory, conduct mining, or develop energy resources. We have lost thousands of jobs because the EPA often imposes unreasonable restrictions on the development of our natural resources.

APPENDIX III:
US DEPARTMENT OF COMMERCE

Responsibilities: To help make American businesses more innovative at home and more competitive abroad.

Annual Budget: 2011 budget authority: $5.7 billion; 2013 budget authority: $9.2 billion.

Employees: 42,000

Bureaus: Economic Development Administration; Census; Economic and Statistical Analysis; International Trade Administration; Bureau of Industry and Security; Minority Business Development Agency; National Oceanic and Atmospheric Admininstration; Patent and Trademark Office; National Institute of Standards and Technology; National Technical Information service; National Telecommunications and Information Administration; Public Safety Broadband Network.

This Department now has a new initiative: investing in manufacturing communities partnership. I wonder what this new program will cost. This new effort is to reward communities that demonstrate plans to attract and expand manufacturing in their area. I haven't even heard of this program on the news, but it sounds like all you need is a plan to get federal money. You really don't need to accomplish anything.

I cannot imagine why this department needs 42,000 employees to accomplish its primary mission. How is it we lost a million jobs in this country when we had 42,000 people working to create jobs and keep America competitive? I guess the employees of this department have just been in training the last twenty years and maybe next year they will start doing something besides collecting statistics.

APPENDIX IV:
HEALTH AND HUMAN
SERVICES (HHS)

Responsibilities: Medicare; Medicaid; temporary assistance for needy families; foster care and permanency; children's health insurance program; child support enforcement; childcare; social services block grants; and other programs.

Annual Budget: $940 billion

Employees: 73,000 in 2011 and 76,000 in 2013.

Medicare is 56 percent of the budget, and Medicaid is 30 percent of the budget.

I don't know how much money is collected from people and businesses to pay for Medicare because the HHS budget does not show the revenue. I suppose the revenue is collected by the US Treasury and is not set aside to fund Medicare.

The main problem with this agency is that the cost of medical care is too high, and there are a lot of people and businesses that overcharge for services and supplies. You hear stories all the time about wheelchairs that are worth $900 being expensed to Medicare at $1,500. Fraud has been reported at billions of dollars a year.

APPENDIX V:
US DEPARTMENT OF EDUCATION

Responsibilities: This department is responsible for administering education programs and conducting research on education.

Annual Budget: 2011: $68.3 billion, 2013: $69.8 billion, and another $5 billion in one-time funds has been requested for elevating the teaching profession.

Employees: 4,300

Programs: elementary and secondary education: thirty-two programs; special education and rehabilitative services: twenty-two programs; student financial assistance: Pell Grants, Opportunity Grants, Perkins Loans, TEACH, and other programs; higher education programs: fourteen programs; and the Institute of Education Sciences. There are so many programs and initiatives that they are too numerous to list here. The agency claims that over forty programs have recently been eliminated, but you notice that their request for funds has not been reduced.

This agency is definitely a political pawn of President Obama as his name is mentioned over and over again in the department's budget narrative.

APPENDIX VI:
US DEPARTMENT OF HOUSING
AND URBAN DEVELOPMENT

Responsibilities: To provide public housing, rental assistance, and community development and planning. Guarantees mortgage-backed securities.

Annual Budget: 2012: $44.1 billion; section 8 rental assistance of $9.34 billion. In 2012 HUD received an extra $100 million in emergency funding for disaster relief.

Programs: There are too many programs to list in this appendix. Some of the major programs are: rental assistance; section 8; public housing; Native American grants; community development block grants; home investment partnerships; homeless assistance grants; rehabilitation of section 8 properties; elderly housing; disabled housing; FHA; GNMA; and Indian housing loan guarantees.

Employees: 10,600 in 2004

States and counties have offices that duplicate many of the HUD programs. The states also provide some funding for these programs so the real cost of public housing cannot be determined.

APPENDIX VII:
US DEPARTMENT OF STATE

Responsibilities: international relations; implements foreign policy; keeper of the great seal; creates jobs at home by opening markets abroad; helps developing nations establish investment and export opportunities; brings nations together to solve international problems like nuclear smuggling.

Annual Budget: 2010: $27.4 billion

Employees: 11,500 foreign service employees; 31,000 foreign service national employees; and 7,400 civil service employees.

The air wing operates more than 230 aircraft around the world. The air wing missions are counter-narcotics and transportation of state officials.

APPENDIX VIII:
US DEPARTMENT OF THE INTERIOR

Responsibilities: Since 1976 it has been the policy of the United States to retain its public lands in federal ownership. The BLM administers about 247.9 million surface acres. Originally, the General Land Office sold or granted vast tracts of public lands to settlers, homesteaders, veterans, towns, new states, railroads and colleges.

The total area of the fifty United States is 2.3 billion acres. About 1.3 billion acres are not owned by the federal government.

Employees: The Bureau of Land Management had 10,000 employees in 2010. BLM also hires 2000 seasonal employees.

Budget: The BLM budget is about $960 million.

The BLM mission is to sustain the health, diversity, and productivity of public lands for the use and enjoyment of present and future generations.

BIBLIOGRAPHY

Ayn Rand, *Atlas Shrugged* (New York, New York: Signet, 1957).

Henry Weaver, *Mainspring, the story of human progress and how not to prevent it* (Detroit, Michigan: Talbot Books, 1947).

Lawrence G. Foster, *Robert Wood Johnson, The Gentleman Rebel* (State College, PA: Lillian Press 1999).

The American College Dictionary (Syracuse, New York: Random House 1963).

Aaron Sojourner and Michael Reich, "In Favor of Updating the Minimum Wage," *Minneapolis Star and Tribune*, February 24, 2013.

Google – USDOE, February 27, 2013. http://en.wikipedia.org/wiki/United_States_Department of Energy.

Google – USEPA, March 9, 2013. http://www.epa.gov/plan and budget/buget.html.

Google – Department of Commerce FY2013 Budget in Brief, April 22, 2013.
http://www.commerce.gov/.

Google – Department of Education FY2013 Budget, March 9, 2013.
http://www2.ed.gov/programs/fpg/index.html.

Google – HUD FY2013 Budget Authority by Program, February 2013.
https://en.wikipedia.org/.../United_States_Department_of Housing_and_Urban_ Development.

Google – US Department of State, February 5, 2013.
http://en.wikipedia.org/wiki/ United_States_Department_of_State.

Google – Department of the Interior, Bureau of Land Management, March 2013.
http://e.n.wikipedia.org/wiki/ United_States_Department_of_the_Interior.

Google – United States Constitution, August 7, 2009.
http://www.usconstitution.net/const.txt.

Google – HHS, March 2013
www.hhs.gov/budget/hhs_general_budget_justification_ fy2013.pdf.

Google – CIA World Factbook, March 2013.
https://www.cia.gov/library/publications/
the_world_factbook/.

Nice, Deb. News Real Blog. Posted on December 27, 2010 at
8:00 pm.
http://www.newsrealblog.com/2010/12/27/top-10-most-
outrageous-quotes-from-nancy-pelosi/.

www.ingramcontent.com/pod-product-compliance
Lightning Source LLC
Chambersburg PA
CBHW020514290526
45786CB00002B/597